Befitting Your Majesty

**How the Twenty-first Century
Christian Contends With
Cultural Assimilation and the
Re-defining of Christianity**

To: ROGER + JEANNIE

FROM
ALAN + CHERYL

Befitting Your Majesty

How the Twenty-first Century Christian Contends With Cultural Assimilation and the Re-defining of Christianity

Jim Mackey, D.Min.

Shepherd Springs, Inc.
2007 Spindle Top
Duncanville, TX 75137

Befitting Your Majesty:
How the Twenty-first Century Christian Contends With Cultural
Assimilation and the Re-defining of Christianity

Copyright © 2016 Jim Mackey

Published in Duncanville, Texas, by Shepherd Springs, Inc.

ISBN 978-0-9725465-2-2

All Scriptures used are from the NIV and ESV Bible translations unless otherwise noted.

Cover design: David S. Harper

Printed in the United States of America

Table of Contents

Dedication

I want to dedicate this book to the people who were most instrumental in the shaping of my life of service to my God and Father. Each of them made their own significant contribution; and this I certainly know, were it not for them nothing would have been gained for God's Kingdom and honor.

Milton Brown, my Pastor: who took me into his heart and held me close when it seemed like life was coming unraveled and who would not allow my ministry to end.

Sam Sasser, my dear friend: who opened my heart and understanding to previously unimaginable intimacy with Jesus.

Hudson Taylor, my mentor *in absentia:* whose writings shaped my sense of integrity to serve God in honorable ways.

Above all, *Lynette,* my wife of forty-five years: without whose presence there would have been nothing.

I am indebted to you all.

Jim

Preface

There are some advantages to living a long time. Not the least of which is having the opportunity to watch global political, religious and cultural changes evolve before your eyes…the future becoming the present. Another advantage in having lived a long time is the great privilege of being able to travel in well over thirty countries on five continents and see how the Church lives and adapts in varied cultures while attempting to remain true to biblical intent.

Toward the end of the 1960's and into the 1970's I observed a shift in the church's focus and energies as a slow but steady erosion of the most central of biblical meanings took place: a life motivated for God's honor was being replaced by a life lived for our personal gain. The focus of the American church seemed to have become blurred and myopic. In the decades since nothing seems to have turned the tide to any great degree. We may have less focus on personal gain but still have missed the mark in living for God's glory.

In this book I hope to bring some small attention to the church's need to refocus on why we do what we do and why a life lived for His majesty is so important. As an adjunct professor I have repeatedly told my students I had one primary objective: to make them *think.* In like manner, I will consider this manuscript a success if it makes any reader *think* about how we as Christians are to live life; to *think* rather than merely acquiesce to the cultural flow; to *think* about what we do and why we do it. And above all to *think* about whom we are *really* living for.

Living a life that is worthy of God *is not* taking the easy road. It *won't* just happen; it *only* happens with intentionality. But it **must** happen if the church's voice is to have significance.

I do have an apology to make. Throughout my life I have written notes to myself when something I read or heard had extra ordinary impact on my thinking and my behavior. Some of those notes I have used in this book. Unfortunately at that time I wrote them solely for my personal growth and encouragement, and, my notes did not always identify the source. Usually I just noted who said it and little else; years ago I had no idea I would someday quote those persons in a book. In this book I have cited and given credit when possible, but there are a few places without full citation. I must apologize for not being able to give full recognition to whom it is due, but I sincerely and humbly thank them for their wisdom and insights which have greatly helped me on my journey.

I also want to thank Amanda Price for her skilled editing touch. And David Harper for his keen eye to graphics and layout.

Introduction

My reason for writing this book is an attempt to call attention to a divine concept of Christian living that seems to have become all but forgotten in the contemporary defining of Christianity. Simply, God's honor *is supposed to be* the objective of all that followers of Christ do and say. It now appears to have become an afterthought. A brief look at the recent history of the church in America will help to explain what has brought me to this place of concern…and perplexity.

A unique spiritual awakening began in the United States immediately following WWII. From 1945 till 1951, revivalists and healing evangelists with their huge tents moved across the nation; great healing miracles of God were common, tens of thousands were saved, and churches were filled. From 1951 to 1961, many Bible colleges across the nation began expanding as enrollment swelled following the harvest of the earlier revivals. Several new Bible colleges opened. In 1958 till 1970 the Charismatic Renewal began and broke through denominational barriers as people across the United States were being filled with the Holy Spirit in Pentecostal fashion. For almost twenty-five years, the entire focus of American Christendom was on the living God.

In 1967 a shift began that took the eyes of the church off the eternal God and onto self. This shift took the believer's attention away from eternity and refocused it almost exclusively on time. In the 1970s Christian self-help books began to dominate shelf space and conversation; almost overnight attention on the living God was displaced with attention on the living "me." Looking back over the last five decades, the church has disproportionately focused on who I am, how do I understand me, what makes me who I am, my rights, my pain, my need, my right to be happy, my plans, my dreams, and my grief. Christianity is all about me: God's primary concern is to bless me, prosper me, and take care of me.

The popular thesis of Christian writing in the first decade of this shift indicated we had finally come to the great truth that God existed for our comfort and self-esteem. That view of life and living was not shared by the first-century church; the apostles simply would not allow them to slip into such a myopic mind-set. The socio-political-religious culture of the first century seems to have striking parallels with the same cultural biases of this century. It appears the dangers that first-century believers faced are rapidly coming to bear on twenty-first-century believers. These two groups of believers are becoming matching bookends, with two thousand years of church history tucked in between. However, I think those first Christians have much to teach us about how to live a life that honors God rather than a lifestyle that honors myself and resolutely slides into cultural assimilation.

What exactly did the apostolic fathers emphasize? Living life for God's honor and glory—it was all about Him. The emphasis that permeates the NT is a lifestyle with conduct that honors God above any personal gain or benefit—a view almost antithetical to present-day Christendom. Paul seemed to take the lead in making honorable Christian living the primary focus on how to live a kingdom life:

- To the church in Ephesus Paul wrote, "Whatever happens, *conduct yourselves in a manner worthy* of the gospel of Christ" (1:27).
- Again to the Ephesians, "I urge you…to *walk in a manner worthy* of the calling to which you have been called" (4:1).
- To the church in Philippi Paul made it abundantly clear that he hoped never to bring shame or disgrace to his Lord: "My eager desire and hope being that I may never feel ashamed, but that now as ever *I may do honor to Christ in my own person*" (1:20 Moffatt).
- To the church in Colossae, Paul wrote "So that you may *live a life worthy of the Lord* and please him in every way" (1:10).
- To the saints in Thessalonica, "*Walk in a manner worthy* of God who calls you into His own kingdom and glory" (1 Thess. 2:12).
- To Timothy Paul wrote, "I am writing you these instructions so that, if I am delayed, you will know *how people ought to conduct themselves* in God's household, which is the church of the living God" (1 Tim. 3:14–15).

If I believe the Holy Spirit guided and directed what the apostles wrote, *I must believe that the emphasis is in fact that of the Holy Spirit!* Whether written to a collective church community or to an individual, it is easy to see the letters were written to set out the kind of conduct expected from all in the house of God—behavior that brought honor to God and His calling of grace. How we walk with each other, how we talk to each other, how we honor or dishonor God…that is the emphasis!

What the Spirit emphasizes can be summarized like this:

- what life is like once you enter the kingdom of God
- how to relate to God
- how to relate to others in the church
- how to relate to those in the world
- how to stand in the face of persecution
- how to grow into the full stature of Christ
- how to establish kingdom values and kingdom principles

All of this results in a life which honors God. The Holy Spirit is only going to emphasize truth in a way that honors God. It would be completely out of character for the Spirit to make this generation hunger and thirst for a "truth" or "revelation" that discounts or marginalizes the *"truth once for all delivered to the saints."* God's Word *has* to be the standard.

It is not our prerogative, not mine and not yours, to offer men and women a framework of Christian thought that is divergent from what God actually *said* **and** *intended*—no matter how bright a person's mind or how genuine one's sympathies to a cause or group, and certainly no matter how culturally compelling. The further away we move from what God intended, the further away we move from really honoring Him. We may even risk the danger of honoring our new "revelation" more than we honor God.

As we read Scripture and make twenty-first-century application, we must be certain that we neither consciously nor unconsciously redesign our manner of living by:

- *Human sympathy*...displacing God's directives because our sympathy tells us, *"That is not fair! Surely God cannot mean that!"*
- *Personal preferences*...making my experience and my personal convictions the standard of belief and practice for all.
- *Tradition*...according to Jesus that makes the Word of God "of no effect."
- *Disproportionate emphasis*...giving importance to any teaching beyond what the Apostolic Fathers gave it.
- *Cultural norms*...succumbing to worldly culture as acceptable Christian living is as deceptive as the false warmth that settles over a person who is actually freezing to death.

Idiosyncrasies of kingdom language, kingdom practice, and kingdom distinction are slowly vanishing in face of the relentless push of an invading worldly culture formed by human wisdom. The loss of Christian identity is not necessarily the result of violent action; it more commonly happens by careless cultural assimilation. When followers of Christ fail to diligently weigh the issues of life on the scales of eternal consequences (not temporal gain), Christ-like distinction fades into nothingness. Rarely do Christians lose their identity by a head-on assault of deadly persecution; history shows that particular strategy when used by past governments or opposing faiths usually tends to strengthen biblical Christianity.

Paul's charge to *"walk worthy"* is not a hard-nosed merit system or legalistic checklist to be followed in order to earn God's approval. It is a charge for us to live so that God is exalted, honored, and glorified in everything we do; that our manner of life brings no shame to His name. Does *this* honor God? Do we consider what God may think about *this* or *that*? If my Christian worldview is all about me, I may be highly sensitized to what is impacting my personal life but have become quite unaware of what the Spirit is actually saying and doing. Whether I live or die is not even the issue!

All of our actions here on earth can be divided into two categories. Everything we do, say, or think can be defined in one of these two ways: first, those that honor God and second, those that dishonor God. Such is the language of Paul in his continual use of the term *worthy*. That word sets boundaries and limits to our living. We cannot just do anything we like and give no thought as to whether it honors God or not. To stay on track, we must frequently remind ourselves that God does not see as we see!

When Moses became provoked by Israel, he did not obey God's instructions to speak to the rock. He struck the rock twice with his rod. What we see as disobedience God saw as dishonor, "Because you did not trust in me enough to honor me as holy in the sight of the Israelites" (Num. 20:12 NIV).

When Eli refused to exercise parental oversight and control his sons as they served in the priesthood, it brought God's punishment. What we see as parental sloth, God saw as dishonor. "You have honored your sons above me." And God's favor lifted from the house of Eli (1 Sam. 2:9 HCSB).

Each chapter of this book is focused on some vital aspect of our Christian walk—some topic, some truth that is obvious to us all. But behind each truth discussed is a greater, not always obvious truth that deals with the greatest single issue we face as men and women professing to be Christ followers: Will my words, my thoughts, my deeds give honor to God? Am I living in a manner befitting His majesty?

When the angels appeared to shepherds keeping watch over their flocks, as they made the grand announcement of the birth of God's Son, they revealed the grand and eternal principle upon which all of life turns: "Glory to God in the highest, and on earth, peace and good will to men." *The glory goes to God;* the good comes to man.

Let me repeat what the angels said: *the glory goes to God,* the good comes to you and me. *Forever settled in heaven —the glory goes to God alone!*

Not to us, O Lord, not to us, but to your name be the glory…

**"I press upon your heart
this one simple thought—
what an absurdity it is to choose
for our life's object anything that
is shorter lived than ourselves!"**

Alexander Maclaren
In His Presence

· 1 ·

Living in Two Worlds

How do you live in two worlds at the same time? There is inevitable stress, and *genuine* struggle, within the life of Christian believers as they blend together the intricacies of simultaneously living in two polar opposite worlds: citizens of earth and citizens of heaven. The socio-political dynamics of one are in sharp contrast, even conflict, with the religious-theological axioms of the other.

A look at the church's historical struggle with cultural adaptation reveals some poignant parallels that will help today's follower of Christ. Like an invisible magnet, there has been a strong pull of social pressure on believers during the past two thousand years. The power of this pull transcends geography and culture; it is everywhere and in every people group. It is persistent and always present. Followers of Christ are pulled to embrace and engage in the dominant visible culture surrounding them, even though it may conflict with their invisible and transformational identity in Christ. From the first-century believer to the twenty-first-century believer, the conflict is real and sometimes threatening: How do we live *in* this world but not be *of* this world?

The pull of cultural assimilation is not illusory. Contemporary Christianity did not just suddenly appear on the stage of human history disconnected from its significant past; neither can it be fully understood without recognizing the painful process first-century believers endured to gift us with God's revelation in Christ. Though all the apostolic writers of Scripture addressed the genuine dilemma of cultural assimilation, no words are more concise, or clearer, than the words Jesus Himself spoke. In the four gospels and in the book of Revelation, Jesus spoke not only from His divine perspective but also from His human experiences and learned observations, because He also lived in the clutches of two earthly cultures like everyone else in Israel.

The first-century church was surrounded by two powerful cultures, Greek and Roman, each presenting its own unique problems to believers. Specifically in a religious sense, the Greek culture designated kings as being divine, while the Roman culture designated Caesar as being divine. The life of the Messianic Christ challenged both cultures morally and religiously. The cultural-religious environment of John's apocalyptic writing, the Revelation, becomes quite clear as John placed greater focus on the culture of Rome than on its counterpart, Greek culture. The seven church letters in Revelation 2–3, and the Revelation as a whole, brought focus to the church's temptation to assimilate into its surrounding Roman culture, doggedly battling invasive compromises wrapped in the lure of the Roman Empire.

The clear heartbeat of the message from Jesus through His messenger John was for the faithful *in any generation* to avoid assimilation into the current culture and to distance themselves from dangerous entanglement. Independent of one's eschatological interpretation of John's work, the Revelation has a rich and meaningful message from the Head of the church that is transgenerational and transcultural; it is a message for every person in every century who reads the book. The message from Jesus identifies two issues common to every believer in the first century and that are becoming *more relevant* to believers in the twenty-first century:

1. being persecuted for their distinctive Christian beliefs
2. being tempted to assimilate into the dominant current culture

During the last half of the first century, these seven churches of Asia Minor[1] (present-day Turkey) lived under immediate Roman rule where Caesar was recognized as god. The Romans had no problem with citizens believing in multiple gods as long as they worshiped Caesar as their preeminent god; to do otherwise was considered treasonous and disruptive to the state's harmony. Since true followers of Christ would worship only one God, conflict with Rome was inevitable.

---

[1] Revelation 2–3

References to the throne of God are repeated no less than forty times in the Revelation, thereby showing God's comprehensive sovereignty in heaven and on earth. This divine universal sovereignty stands in opposition to the political regimes (Roman or otherwise, ancient or current) that make man or manmade systems the object of worship. For believers there was only one *true* God, and allegiance to Him was inviolate, non-negotiable, and beyond assimilation.

The apostolic writers voiced a common warning. Quite clear in the apocalyptic literature of John, the pastoral epistles of Paul, and the general epistles of Peter is the caution for believers to *not* see assimilation as a quaint irrelevance or mere unwanted interruption. The Christian's world is ordered distinctively different because of the one divine authority who governs it. As such, God's order is expressed in ways that can rarely be understood by human logic. With stark realism the use of kingdom rhetoric poses a life radically different from anything we know on earth.

Not Ancient History, but Contemporary Awareness

So, how do you live in two worlds at the same time? If the two worlds, or kingdoms, are somewhat similar, the task is not necessarily unappealing. However, the two worlds or kingdoms in which the believer lives are completely antithetical to each other. To get a fuller picture of this dilemma, a baseline sense of rule and authority must be established for Christians. Believers and nonbelievers alike understand the gist of Jesus' words: "Render unto Caesar what is Caesar's and unto God what is God's."[2] The demarcation between God's rule and place versus the rule and place of societal politics is not imaginary for true believers; it is very real.

The early disciples understood that some dimensions of life belong to God alone. Upon release from prison for preaching the gospel, they declared, "We must obey God rather than man!"[3] Does this mean *all* things political are necessarily evil mandates requiring ungodly assimilation? No. Paul's lengthy discourse in Romans 13 makes clear that governing authorities have been established by God in order to affirm and maintain civil order, to hold accountable and punish evildoers, to watch over and promote justice.[4]

However, Peter's response above (Acts 5) makes clear that the authority and rule of God supersedes if the rule of man is contradictory to His authority. Unfortunately, trying to accept and honor *both* the rule of God and the rule of man may result in severe consequences; in some cases doing both is not at all possible. The disciples honored and obeyed the superior law of God (which resulted in imprisonment), yet also honored the law of man by willfully submitting to the

---

[2] Matthew 22:15–22, Mark 12:13–17, Luke 20:20–26
[3] Acts 5:27–29
[4] Romans 13:1–7

government's authority without protestation. Though Paul protested his treatment in the jail at Philippi (imprisoned because he honored the commands of God), his rightful demands for correct treatment by the jailor were made in strict accordance with Roman law (i.e., he insisted man's laws must also be honored).[5]

One of the objectives in apostolic writings was to forewarn believers that persecution was to be anticipated if they resisted socio-political assimilation into Roman culture… but resist they must. Within the message to these first-century readers, Christ sends a message pertinent to believers in each successive generation; that includes today's church. His message is twofold: first, each person must see *their* own present day socio-political government entity as substituted for what is pictured by Roman rule; second, yielding to the pressure of assimilation into the dominant culture will bring a believer into direct conflict with kingdom principles.

It plays out in this fashion:

- The imperial cult of Rome symbolizes man's historical culture of worshiping himself above God and demanding allegiance to his self-authorized and self-empowered perceptions.

---

[5] Acts 16:22–40

- This stands in sharp contrast with heaven's throne room, which becomes a visual mandate that: 1) God alone be worshiped; 2) His rule must be embraced; and 3) His name be exalted.
- The throne room of John's heaven shows the eternal sovereign rule of God in heaven and on earth, while Roman rule is *the symbolic canvas upon which is portrayed the rule of man in every successive generation and every culture.*

In order to live in two world kingdoms at the same time, boundaries must be set; one culture must ultimately supersede the other. They cannot be equals. John's throne in heaven has a distinguishing feature; it is not the chair itself but the One sitting on it. Thus in Christian culture, the focus on the Ruler is to focus on *more than* His place; it equally embraces His *qualifications to rule*: His character and His sovereignty. No Caesar (or ruler by any other title) of any generation can compare.

The ultimate question thus becomes, "Who will I allow the greater rule in my life: God's eternal Christ on the throne in heaven, or earth's transient Caesar?" Sorting out the answers to these two questions, first, "How do you live in two worlds at the same time?" and second, "Who will I allow the greater rule in my life?" leads to an unavoidable confrontation of cultures. It always has.

As you read any church historian who wrote about first-century believers, you find the early saints never discovered any holy-grail solution that would resolve the tension between cultural assimilation and cultural disassociation, especially about money and wealth, or moral purity and sexual license. Theologies of asceticism and rejection were never far away; theologies of opulence and prosperity weren't either. They still aren't.

Present Landscape for Christian Culture

As the social-political-religious landscape continues to be in a state of flux in the twenty-first century, Christianity's influence in America wanes. Common seasonal icons (e.g., images for Easter, Christmas, and Thanksgiving) with their traditional pageantry bearing Christian overtones are being suppressed by political correctness, accompanied by judicial activism and rejection. In rather quick fashion, Christians are becoming the new minority.

However, the decline of influence by Christianity largely rests on its own willingness to sacrifice its distinctiveness on the altar of assimilation and acceptance. It seems as if the thing Christians fear more than anything else is being different! Culturally accommodating Christianity is assuredly on the rise. Yet, the Head of the church says distinctiveness is not optional for life in His kingdom. It is required.

For the church the need for adaptation on some level is essential in order to have any social impact, and possibly for the church's own survival. But how far do we go? Two extremes need to be avoided. The first is the bunker mentality, so focused on separation from the world the church becomes isolated and judgmental and ultimately is socially ignored. The second is the cheap grace mentality, which is so focused on not offending anyone it minimizes the distinctive beliefs and praxis essential to "Christ-follower" identity; the church thereby becomes transformationally impotent.

In many areas global Christians are trying to put as much visible space between themselves and American Christianity as possible so as to avoid being found guilty by association because of politics supported by the West. Some are even distancing themselves from the increasing liberal slant to morals and ethics, which are taking deep roots in the American church. None is more obvious than the global Anglican-Episcopal Church's open rejection of the American Episcopal Church's openness to homosexuality as a viable Christian-life alternative.

How Much Adaptation Is Too Much?

Christians must adapt to live in this world—but how much? To avoid being cut off from an active role in the prevailing culture (and thereby having no voice), do we accept the language and value system of the common culture? Yet the more we accept the language and value system of the ruling culture, to that degree we accelerate marginalization and growing ineffectiveness of kingdom principles and values.

For example, if the prevalent culture defines "sin" as a disease or dysfunction, something to be treated by medicine or psychology, and Scripture defines the same act as "sin," and it is to be "treated" with repentance and restoration. Christians must make the choice of assimilating into transient mainstream values or retaining their kingdom value system, which is based on God's character and redemptive plan.

If Christianity is not different, what does it have to offer? To adapt too little results in cultural irrelevance; we will have isolated ourselves as paragons of holier-than-thou elitists. To adapt too much results in the same thing: cultural irrelevance. We will have ceased to exist as salt and light, providing nothing of redemptive substance to people who need it the most.

Non-believers and politically correct theorists do not of themselves determine the outcome of Christianity's future; decisions by Christian churches themselves contribute to the outcome. Decades of in-fighting over peripheral differences (e.g., the distorted prosperity gospel) and decades of longing to be "liked" (e.g., the seeker-friendly message) have not been without consequence. The consequences have not always been immediately apparent, but they have been damaging. Since Christianity allows for broad interpretation of its dogma, there are no universally accepted definitions of what exactly is the "good news;" and no universally accepted strategies of how to share the "good news." Consequently, the church's influence slowly fades into a collection of religious groups pushing their own agenda.

Everything to Everybody...Redemptive Assimilation

Do the apostle Paul's words, "I have become all things to all men,"[6] open the door for wider flexibility and adaptation into the ruling culture? I suggest to those who are legalists it should be read as such—an open door to more grace. Paul is a good example of becoming more flexible in non-essentials and non-sinful differences which are not core truths of the gospel message. Rigidly promoted personal preferences and doctrinal nonessentials are assuredly counterproductive to the gospel.

More precisely, the context of verses preceding Paul's words in verse 22 show that he is not presenting a strategy of *cultural assimilation* but a strategy of *redemptive assimilation*. Paul's method to advance the gospel was to be all things to as many as possible; that is not a case of chameleon-like

---

[6] 1 Corinthians 9:22

inconsistency or hypocrisy. It is Paul's ability, in grace and freedom, to share something in common with everybody:

* to the Jews, "I became like a Jew…to win them" (20).
* to those not having the law, "I became like them…to win them" (21).
* to the weak, "I became weak…to win them" (22).

His *redemptive assimilation* accepted things noncriminal or sinful—things not contrary to God's moral law; things not contrary to sound doctrine; things that would not violate the disciplines of Christ. *Simply, freedom to assimilate has limits*. Neither Paul nor any other apostle would forsake core teachings of Christ so as to adapt to heresies in order to win the heretic. In fact, almost one-half the NT is written to warn the church about encroaching heresies. The apostles fought against heresy; they did not adapt to it to win the propagators. The apostles did not abandon the revelation of Christ to make the Gnostics feel welcome.

Contemporary religious conflicts and cultures have to be considered as well; it is not just a first-century story. Today Paul would be warning believers against assimilating into "Chrislam."[7] This religious syncretism of Christianity and

---

[7]I have selected to pinpoint Chrislam over other possible cultural and religious conflicts simply because of personal experience. Since the mid-1990s I have been actively working in nations where the growth and tensions of Islam are predominant and the compromise of blending it with Christianity is real.

Islam, which began resurgence in the 1980s, is not widely accepted. However, it is of genuine concern, particularly in nations whose predominant religion is Islam, where social peace is gained at the loss of doctrinal purity. Paul's few words, "all things to all men," have unfortunately been used to support this kind of extreme missionary accommodation.

When Is Christianity Not Christianity?

The current "insider movement" runs parallel to the rise of Chrislam. Methodology of the insider movement is designed to allow persons to remain in their culture while being covert followers of Jesus. Assuredly this will all but alleviate persecution, but the compromising synergetic belief system that results is not that person's original religion, nor is it biblical Christianity. Today's insider movement is an attempt to reach other cultures and other religions with the gospel of Christ, without requiring them to forsake their national culture. By itself that is not necessarily problematic; the danger arises when there is no requirement made for them to forsake their *religion*.

To take Paul's words beyond his meaning and make them a tool of evangelism for the current "Chrislam" or "insider movement" is a slippery slope at best. It is essential to remember the apostolic writers paid little attention to, and gave little space to, peripheral cultural differences. *But they were adamantly opposed to violations of core truth, those revelations by the Spirit that made Christianity what it is.*

Today this method is most commonly found in attempts to convert Muslims to Christianity. But the insider movement basically ignores matters of doctrine. Thus, hybrid "Chrislam" just is not acceptable; Christian doctrine cannot be avoided and still remain Christian. Islam does not just minimize basic Christian doctrines; it eviscerates Christian doctrine. In Islam:

- Jesus is not God.
- Jesus is not divine.
- Jesus did not come as God in the flesh to redeem humankind (Hollywood versus the Bible belt).
- It is blasphemous to say Jesus is the Son of God.
- It is blasphemous to recognize Jesus as Savior.
- It denies that Jesus was crucified.
- It denies that Jesus even died; Allah translated Him.
- To worship Jesus as Lord is heresy.

Simply put, the Jesus of the Bible and the Jesus (Isa) of the Qur'an are not the same. The incompatibility (i.e., the inability to assimilate with Islam) is further revealed in Islam's eschatology:

- Jesus will return as a radical Muslim.
- Upon His return, Jesus will make a pilgrimage to Mecca.
- Jesus will enforce Islamic *shariah* law around the world.
- Jesus will be a global teacher of Islam.
- Jesus will abolish Christianity.

While Muslims may declare Jesus is a prophet, they number Him as only one among thousands—all subservient to Mohammed. Their Jesus is not the centrality of life, as the Christian Jesus is to Christians. To the Muslim, Mohammed is central, and Jesus is peripheral.

The apostle James wrote a great truth about the power and role of the tongue, which I believe has broader application, an application appropriate to Chrislam: "Can both fresh water and saltwater flow from the same spring?[8] My brothers, can a fig tree bear olives, or a grapevine bear figs? Neither can a salt spring produce fresh water." The gospel of Jesus Christ is a message of hope to everyone who hears and believes. Everyone. That cannot be said of Islam. Salvation in Islam is works based, with an unpredictable outcome. You may or may not have done enough to enter Islam's heaven. The only *sure way* into Islam's heaven is to kill someone in a holy war (jihad) or to be killed in jihad. Hope, hopelessness. Fresh water, salt water.

There are such doctrinal contradictions between the two religions that assimilation from a Christian perspective is impossible. Chrislam is impossible…except for members and proponents of the insider movement. The actions of the insider movement are more than a compromise of Christianity; they are abandonment of the gospel. Redemp-

---

[8] James 2:11–12

tive assimilation meant something entirely different to Paul
than that which they propose.

Challenging, but Not Impossible

The world is at war. It is a conflict being fought on all fronts.
It is a multifaceted war of cultures, and increasingly a war
against Christianity. Everything is in flux:

- one form of politics versus another
- one genre of music versus another
- to tattoo and pierce or not tattoo and pierce
- *Ad finitum*

It would not be far amiss to consider culture the yeast in
the loaf: it will permeate everything. Living in two worlds at
the same time is a genuine challenge for Christians; sure
answers and true direction are a must. But only the Spirit is
wise enough to lead and guide us. We can no longer fill the
gaps in our understanding by defaulting to our own comfort
zone: personal culture and upbringing.

The culture of heaven must take prominence.

"We must remember that culture communicates. The question is what does it communicate and how clear is the message? We must remember that the gospel is supra cultural in its origin and essence but cultural in its interpretation and application."

Aubrey Malphurs
A New Kind of Church

· 2 ·

The Role of Culture in Shaping Christian Life

For the past two decades in America, there has been a persistent call from both church leaders and regular church members for the church to regain its relevance in national and global societies; change is urgently needed. Why? Increasing evidence suggests that the church has lost its distinctiveness as a holy people and has unwittingly embraced the dominant common culture or too sympathetically embraced the culture of political correctness.

Simply put, the church has too eagerly assimilated to cultural dynamics without enough careful analysis of the true cost. Obviously, culture matters. Culture influences music, art, politics, history, finances, style, fashion, *ad finitum*; remember culture is like the leaven in bread, it permeates *everything*. It even influences interpretation of the Bible (a later chapter). The place *and* influence of culture in the formation of the believer's doctrine and praxis just cannot be minimized.

But if culture is so important and so influential, how do you define it? As a working term for us, *culture* will be used in reference to the distinction of language, customs, values, beliefs, experience, history, and preferences. In other words, *what people **use** in giving meaning and substance to their life.*

The simple passing of time changes the way we may identify a culture. Geopolitical events influence and modify people's culture; economic pleasures, or deficiencies, have direct powers on the mind-set and practice of living out life, thereby *creating a culture.* People born in a certain time period experience and are shaped by circumstances and global happenings that may never happen exactly the same way again in another time period. A generation of people who have known relative peace within their land will have a culture of values and beliefs very different from those people who have lived firsthand through the horror of war. People who were raised with a democratic form of government have a culture of beliefs and practices usually quite different than people raised under a dictatorship.

But from all these elements people emerge with values and beliefs that have genuine influence on their view of life. So in the broader view of culture, from nation to nation, there is no universal unifying culture that covers *all* details in a community's life...no oneness of *all* customs, *all* beliefs, *all* history, or *all* preferences.

When religion is the engine that pulls the train, the complexities intensify. Even the regional quadrants of my own country (the United States) pose such differing religious options in life choices for believers the emphases vary from one region to another. The church in New England may look and sound culturally different from the church in the Deep South, yet both are truly Christian. In this nation, though we may all call ourselves Americans, geographical differences in culture are present. Merely crossing the street in a metropolitan city may take you into an entirely different ethnic, racial, or religious culture. So extensive is cultural influence to the human race that these variants prove to be of global concern when defining what is and what is not "Christian."

Collective Culture

The topography of Christendom seems to change every thirty to forty years. Some change is openly welcomed, but historically people seem to require a crisis of some measure before change is embraced. In recent years several tragic events have altered our world—events that cannot be undone, change that will never be reversed. But one undeniable result is that when believers are hard pressed by life, they always renew and reevaluate their kingdom orientation.

Beginning with the first generation of Christians and into the present twenty-first-century generation of Christians, some distinct similarities of these two church eras are worth noting. Both the historical and contemporary churches were (are) compelled to confront cultural assimilation by social, political, and religious pressures. Both generations were (are) challenged:

• with political and social persecution,
• with an invasion of immorality,
• by wrongly emphasizing peripheral truth, and
• to redefine Christianity.

These are so interwoven that it is not always easy to clearly define cause and effect, which came first, what caused what. It is almost as if these two generations of Christians are matching bookends of church history: what the first-generation church experienced, the last-generation church will experience. Let's look at the similarities of these two.

Political and Social Persecution

Each era had/has to face persecution for their belief system. What we now see emerging is but a faint glimpse of what is to come. Globally, stages of persecution against the church are quite varied, ranging from the early stages of being a social nuisance, to being hated and vilified, to the more accelerated stages of criminalizing, imprisonment, and death. The church in America is being compelled to revise its sanitized view of how safe it really is to be Christian. It is discovering that persecution is no longer isolated to foreign soil.

I believe in my lifetime, persecution of Christians in America will rival that of believers in the first-century church. The day is quickly approaching where saints must make decisions about embracing the cross or embracing their culture. As the church becomes more a center for motivational rallies and pep talks, she becomes less and less prepared for the inevitable. As it is said of the next terrorist attack, so with persecution; it is not *if* it will happen, but *when*.

The Invasion of Immorality into the Church

Each society in these two church eras had/has become a culture dominated by sexual desire; the sheer magnitude of its influence is astonishing. The first-century church arose during the time when sexual purity had been long abandoned. Greek and Roman cultures embraced homosexuality as common practice. Divorce was out of control, and having ten to twenty marriages in these cultures was not at all shocking.

Neither has the church of the twenty-first century been immune to such immoral vices, natural or unnatural. Homosexuality has such political, judicial, and cultural clout that it has become mainstream. Having lost the sense of what God made natural, even the church has begun to make the unnatural the new normal. Ten to twenty marriages is not likely to be found today like it was in the first century, but we have replaced it with our own cultural failures. Immorality and impurity have become blasé.

Recently I had lunch with a good friend of mine, an influential bishop in Dallas. He caught me off guard with these words: "Across the city, in church or out of church, 70 percent of our young women who have babies are not married. Our mega-churches are nothing more than entertainment centers. We don't care about how people live; we just want them to entertain us and make us feel good." I can neither confirm nor refute his observation, but it was at the least very disconcerting.

But what about church leaders—are they struggling with moral issues? The same week I met with the bishop, I met with a clinical psychologist who works in the Dallas metroplex, and she stunned me even more. "Jim, if you could gather data from all clinics and therapists in the metroplex regarding the number of *church leaders* with drug or alcohol abuse problems they are counseling, you would be amazed. Multiply that number by four. Then you would have a much closer picture of the magnitude of this growing problem among *church leaders* in the area." I cannot refute her observation either but certainly found it equally disconcerting.

Almost every week some kind of sexual abuse of a parishioner by a church leader is uncovered and reported; if not that, then a secret sexual lifestyle of clergy involved in affairs or perversion is in the headlines. It is not naïve to hope that the church would be different, because it *should be expected* to be different.

Wrongly Emphasized Peripheral Truth

What we preach and teach does not necessarily help the situation. Not long ago I was invited to be the guest teacher for a week at a local Bible college. The class was Advanced Leadership and Pastoral Studies. One morning I asked the 110 students to identify the top three messages emphasized in the church of their generation. They *unanimously* agreed on the number-one message of their generation: prosperity. I then asked them to define this number-one Christian message of their generation. *Unanimously* they defined it as "money and financial gain."

To complicate matters further, they were from twenty-two different countries of the world. Just think what we as the American church have *exported* around the world. While we have preached peace and prosperity, the world has been coming unraveled. Men and women who have been called and trusted to guard and feed the people of God have a decision to make. What will be the emphasis of my message? The Psalmist sets the pattern for much more than his personal testimony when he writes, "I will declare the decrees of the Lord."[1] God's Word must be declared. God's point of view must be embraced. What the Spirit

---

[1] Psalm 2:7

emphasizes, I must emphasize. The first-century church was not picture perfect as it struggled with the allure of the mysterious and its so-called privileged, secret information promoted by Gnosticism. From the book of Acts to the book of the Revelation, almost every writer takes time to address this invasive problem.

In an age of societal upheaval, failure to adhere to the truth of Scripture as inviolate will result in injury to the relevance of the church...in any century.

The Redefining of Christianity

Both the first-century and the twenty-first century-church had/have to come to grips with how much do we assimilate into our culture without losing our identity. For the past decade we all have observed the cultural redefining of Christianity. The pressure to be *inclusive* has been unrelenting. But it is not an inclusiveness based upon an invitation of God's grace. "Whoever believes on the Lord Jesus Christ shall be saved."[2] Nor is it inclusiveness based upon repentance. "Your sins are forgiven. Now go and sin no more."[3]

Rather it is an inclusiveness that does not require transformation or the abandonment of sinful behavior. We have redefined Christianity with so much inclusiveness that

---

[2] Romans 10:13
[3] John 8:11

transformation has been made optional and holy living has become unnecessary. The new definition of Christianity embraces everything at the cost of nothing.

Culture and Decisions

We bring our culture into the church and its parachurch ministries; they come to bear on our decision making and strategic planning. In a very real sense, culture gives meaning and continuance to church life, so much so that a dynamic tension evolves: Christianity influences culture, and culture influences Christianity. Though we may, with all good intentions, suggest that twenty-first-century believers need to live like the first believers did, that in itself can be both falsely encouraging and unnecessarily condemning.

Francis Schaeffer said in his book *The Church at the End of the Twentieth Century*, "Not being able, as times change, to change under the Holy Spirit is ugly. The same applies to church polity and practice."

The challenge is to uncover the eternal truth (not the cultural truth) of kingdom living that supersedes generations and then make a contemporary application. Far too many believers in America need an adjusted worldview that will honestly recognize that the gospel is not an American commodity. We live in a world with complex cultures and political diversities that requires an ability to separate the gospel from American culture and American politics.

Simply, the gospel is not an extension of democracy. We do not have the freedom to judge global believers through the expectation that once they accept the gospel, their acceptance of democracy will follow. The two have no mutual requirements.

In several of the countries where I travel, to say you are an American is interpreted to mean you are a Christian…and in a few places to say you are a Christian is interpreted to mean you must be an American. God help us! Contemporary believers need to learn, on an international scale, how to translate the meaning of the gospel into their local culture *without transforming the gospel.*

The "how" of Christian living does have a very definitive cultural and geopolitical lifespan; what influences me today will be gone tomorrow and a new influence takes its place. My analysis starts all over: How does this practice fit into my kingdom principles? Does it fit at all? Does part of it fit? Life is the crucible where two disparate cultures come to an uneasy and cautious cooperation; how does this decision impact both cultures in which I live?

Personal Culture

God is not looking for people who are pristine and uninfluenced by this fallen world; to think so is beyond naiveté. He is not searching for people who have been isolated from life to serve Him. He is looking for real people, living in a real world, who can in real fashion bring kingdom realities into their native culture. It is *eternity invading time.*

Every experience you have had (good or bad) and every person who has influenced your thinking (right or wrong) has played a role in preparing you to serve God in your natural earthly culture. Many of the things we wish were different in our lives, such as,

- "I wish I had not been born in a small town,"
- "I wish I had not been born poor,"
- "I wish I had been born in the city,"
- "I wish I had not been abandoned," and
- "I wish I had not been abused"

are the things we would like to undo about ourselves, but simultaneously they are the very things God strategically plans on using. Even if they are painful, tragic, abhorrent, even inexcusable...placed in the hands of God they become extraordinary, with eternal value.

Your culture becomes the baseline of your Christian living and your service to the kingdom and the advance of the gospel. Allowing the Spirit of God to touch all the components and pieces of your life is to elevate your history into a new dimension of divine significance and purpose. Your culture is inseparable from you and becomes part of the pressure points God uses to mold you into a vessel of His own choosing.

I find it interesting to see how God infused three cultural elements into Paul's life to mold him into the most uniquely qualified preacher, apostle, and teacher of the first century so he might be used as God's voice to the Gentiles:

1. He was of *Jewish* descent from the tribe of Benjamin. Paul's Jewish heritage allowed him to begin his ministry in each city with a ready-made audience. He could have preached on the street corner but didn't have to. All he had to do was go to the local synagogue and begin to teach/preach, revealing Christ in all the Scripture; this audience was educated in the Scripture and used to religious discussion. It seems that Paul saw his Jewish heritage as an asset; before King Agrippa (Acts 26), the chief captain (Acts 21), and the mob in Jerusalem (Acts 22), the first thing he declared in his defense was, "I am a Jew."

2. He had *Roman citizenship.* He was born into the political privileges of the Roman state (a resident of Tarsus) and on several occasions used these rights to his advantage. As a Roman citizen, he pleaded his own case before the Roman governors Felix and Festus, and as a Roman citizen he appealed his case from their court to Caesar himself. No other apostle could have done that! It was this appeal that opened the doors for a trip to Rome

(albeit as a prisoner) and that brought the entire Praeto-rian Guard under his witness. Paul said, "These chains have advanced the Gospel."[4]

3. He was accustomed to *Greek culture* with its focus on education and wisdom; Paul was born and raised in Tarsus, a Greek city of Asia Minor with a large university. Tarsus was one of the three major university cities of the world at that time, along with Athens and Alexandria. At some time in his youth, his parents moved to Jerusalem —another city with a different culture yet also providing a university education. Simply put, Paul was a city boy, exposed to education and international cultures. He was not raised on the farm with dirt under his fingernails or near the sea with the smell of fish on his hands.

No other apostle had this sort of triple advantage. With this unique cultural blend as his background, no other apostle was more qualified to be God's voice to the Gentiles than Paul. The other apostles were mostly Galilean fishermen, tradesmen, and laborers. Certainly used of God in their own right, but not one of them was as prepared as Paul to stand before governors, kings, senators, and Caesars. Paul could stand in the cities of the world and speak to people of any culture, with any education, and do so with confidence and without embarrassment.

---

[4] Philppians 1:12,13

Paul's Jewish heritage and culture, his Roman citizenship and culture, his exposure to Greek culture and education, combined to prepare him for a lifelong ministry to Gentile nations in a way that far surpassed any other first-century church leader. For Paul to minimize the influence of his blended culture would have limited his usefulness and effectiveness among the people groups God placed him with.

So it is with you, and so it is with me. God does not eradicate a person's past cultural influences; He uses them. God does not begin using *only* one's cultural influences in the present, as if *only* what transpires post-conversion is usable. Paul's model suggests God will actively bring to bear diverse experiences throughout our formative years as instruments to make the vessel He needs today.

"Preach the gospel at all times and when necessary use words."

Francis of Assis

· 3 ·

Citizens of Heaven

The visible realities of this world appeal to all of our senses as they challenge invisible realities. How do you live in two worlds at the same time when one world is so obviously real and the other so obviously intangible? It was this very real dilemma that created the backdrop for the apostle Paul's letter to Philippi. His charge to them was "Above all, you must live as citizens of heaven, conducting yourselves in a manner worthy of the gospel."[1] His encouraging reminder was that they not become too engrossed in this world because they were in fact aliens just passing through. Their real citizenship was in heaven.[2]

Through the whole of this epistle, Paul pointedly calls attention to the dilemma of dual citizenship for believers. It exists and is undeniable. In a natural sense they saw one form of citizenship modeled every day, the earthly dominant culture of Rome. What they needed was a model of the invisible citizenship that would make their task of avoiding assimilation into the dominant culture around them some-what easier. That is, they needed an authentic measuring stick against which they could gauge themselves to see

---

[1] Philippians 1:27 NLT
[2] Philippians 3:20

how well they were living for their King. The city in which they lived removed some of the wonder and guesswork on how to live in a world they had never been to or seen.

Philippians was written to saints who lived in a military outpost of the Roman Empire. The city was founded in 356 BCE by the king of Macedon, Philip II. But in 42 BCE, the city was captured by Roman armies. As a Roman colony, the language of Rome was spoken; Roman dress was worn; Roman customs observed; and all political titles were Roman. These transplanted Romans had no intention of assimilating with the local people…they were Romans. This military colony and outpost existed to protect Roman interests in the region.

Though all these events took place some ninety-plus years before the writing of this epistle, they still had particular impact on key elements of Paul's writing. Using the visible models of his own life and that of the Romans who reformed their city, Paul clearly emphasizes the kingdom's pattern of distinctive difference. The apostle's portrait between the saints of God and people of other cultures is not a suggestion that believers look to their dominant culture in order to find out how to live as citizens of heaven. It will not be found in a tit-for-tat copying of any current culture of any century: title for title, dress for dress, practice for practice, etc. He is only using the Romans as a pattern of having *a focused commitment to being distinct…and loyal.*

The question remains, why this letter to this people? This Roman outpost offered the perfect example for *unwavering non-assimilation*. There is one overriding theme to this epistle, not several. The apostolic intent is to capture the attention of the church at Philippi and in no uncertain terms, compel them to see themselves as distinctively different, as saints of God, from other peoples and other cultures.

Though using multiple examples and illustrations (which may appear as themes to some), Paul will accomplish his end by directing their understanding to the powerful work of God being done by the Spirit. First, the Spirit is enabling them to live differently (to think and act differently) and second, to see the future differently (to bring eternity into the present). His writing is not about peripheral issues, which may change in each generation, but addresses core issues of living and sorting out life as a different people.

A Different Identity: Slaves and Saints

To quickly read over Paul's salutation as insignificant, or to see it as merely a common greeting, would be to miss the foundation upon which he is going to build the full scope of his purpose in writing them at all. The apostle uses two terms that set the stage for what is to come: servants and saints. "Paul and Timothy, *servants* of Christ Jesus, to all the *saints* of Christ Jesus who are at Philippi..."[3]

---

[3] Philippians 1:1

In his address to his friends, as Paul speaks of himself he uses the word *doulos*, which is much more than a *"servant."* It in fact carries meaning even beyond the Philippians more widely used term *slave*—the premise of Paul is in fact reference to a *"bond slave."* The clearest picture of what the apostle is conveying can be traced to his knowledge of the Torah (e.g., Ex. 21:6). From his opening statement, Paul immediately challenges the thinking of this church; he immediately confronts the common culture they have unwittingly embraced as he awakens them to have a renewed sense of *their difference.*

For centuries, slavery and slave laws in the Mediterranean region had been culturally invasive, and this church would have known them quite well. Here are some of the slave laws that influenced and guided this time and culture:

- "There can be no friendship, nor justice, toward inanimate things; indeed not even a horse or an ox, nor yet toward a slave. For master and slave have nothing in common; a slave is a living tool, just as a tool is an inanimate slave."
- "Whatever a master does to a slave, undeservedly, in anger, willingly, unwillingly, in forgetfulness, after careful thought, knowingly, unknowingly, is judgment, justice, and law."
- "The only difference between a slave and a beast or a farmyard cart is that a slave happens to be able to speak."

- By law a slave was considered not a person, but a thing, with no rights whatsoever. He could not marry but could cohabit; however, any child born to the union belonged to the master. He was a "thing" with nothing in the world to call his own, not even himself.[4]

The estimated population of the Roman Empire during Paul's time was approximately 300 million people, of which some 60 million were slaves; it is a sobering thought to think that 20 percent of the populace would be in some level of servitude. Keen sensitivity to that obvious cultural reality is exactly what Paul was trying to arouse within them, with a specific kingdom application in mind.

His thought gets closer to home for them because they were fully aware that over one-half the people who comprised the church surrounding the Mediterranean Sea (southern Europe, Asia Minor, and North Africa) were either present or former slaves.

What would a slave want more than anything else? Freedom. Yet, Paul is reminding his friends that he voluntarily gave up his freedom to become a slave! A slave with no rights! To Paul this is not some interesting Sunday school lesson. It is real life and real living; to him it is *the essence of being in Christ Jesus.*

---

[4] These came from notes I have taken through the years from various works of William Barclay.

What was apparently a cultural designation of great humili-
ation, being a slave, Paul was willing to take as his highest
honor. What they were trying to disassociate from, trying to
leave in their past, he was embracing, and thereby used
his own life as an illustration for them to emulate. Paul saw
the designation of *servant/slave of Christ Jesus* as a title
of highest honor. A Latin expression captures Paul's heart
well: *Illi servire esi regnare*, which may be translated, "To be
his slave is to be a king."[5]

The second word he used seems so common to religion,
and to Scripture, as to be easily, and wrongly, minimized:
saints. We toss it around with such casualness and indifference that it has very little meaning. We relegate the word
to some eschatological moment in some distant future, but
with no present-day significance. Saints in heaven...yes.
Here and now...never.

At this point, Paul interweaves OT Jewish culture and dogma into their Greek culture and understanding. The Greek
word he uses for "saint" is *hagios*, *usually* translated holy,
or consecrated. Paul continues his OT thought by apply-
ing this dynamic to their present Christocentric life. The OT
counterpart for holy/saint was two interchangeable words,
qodesh (sacred, consecrated, dedicated) and *qadowsh* (to
pronounce holy, hallowed, consecrated).

---

[5] A Latin phrase from The Book of Common Prayer published in the mid-1500's.

Each term carries the basic idea of being *different* from other things—in some sense *set apart* from other things. So even while we use the weaker English translation "saints," with clear focus Paul lays his foundation for the entire letter: the Philippians are to exist, function, think, and live as *distinctively different people.*

To better see this, note a few examples in the OT for use of the word holy/saints:

- The priests were to be *holy* unto their God (Lev. 21:6). They were to be different from other men.
- The tithe was to be *holy* unto God (Lev. 27:30). The tithe was different from other things.
- The central part of the temple was the *Holy* Place (Ex. 26:33). It was different from all other places in the temple.
- Israel was a *holy* nation (Ex. 19:6). They were to be different from any other nation.

Here is the divine pattern for the people of God. Just as the Jews-Israel had been holy-different, now the saints-church are to be holy-different. So when Paul addresses the Philippians as "the holy ones in Christ Jesus,"[6] he is reminding them they have been called out to be the people who are *different.* The remainder of his letter is real-life application of

---

[6] Philippians 1:1

how being in Christ requires a distinctively different manner of life than that lived by everyone around us.

A Different Citizenship: Heaven Not Rome

The Roman Empire had both senatorial provinces, those in which the Roman senate appointed the governor, and imperial provinces, those in which Caesar appointed the governor. Correspondingly along the frontier of the Roman Empire were other military outposts or colonies like Phillippi. But these were more than just outposts; each colony was a "little Rome." They were fiercely proud of their Roman citizenship: 1) Latin was spoken by the people deployed there; 2) Roman dress was worn; 3) Roman customs were followed; 4) Roman festivals were observed; and 5) political offices were given Roman titles.

Wherever they were located, these colonies were stubbornly and unalterably *Roman*. They would *never* have dreamt of being assimilated to the people among whom they were set, or changed by the people who came to live among them. They were parts of Rome, miniature cities of Rome, and they never forgot it! In his first visit to Philippi, Paul encountered Lydia by the river, then followed his encounter with the young woman having a spirit of divination; when arrested, the charges against him were based upon the local citizenry's unshakable commitment to their Roman heritage. "He advocates customs that are not lawful for us as *Romans* to accept or practice."[7]

To the different people in Philippi, the apostle uses this visible cultural commitment of citizenship loyalty as an object lesson for the church. "Our citizenship is in heaven."[8] His reminder is clear: the believer's citizenship is based on relationship, not on geographical location. His teaching did some powerful things:

- It reaffirmed their identity—who they were. They were not citizens of Italy, Greece, Egypt, or even Israel. As *different people*, their citizenship was not one of national loyalties, but kingdom loyalties; they were God's people, not Caesar's.
- It brought eternity into the present. Their citizenship was not only an eschatological reality; it was a present reality. As *present-day* citizens of heaven, their current life and conduct on earth was to be distinctively different from the culture around them.

The pervasive thought of Paul in Philippians is that being "in Christ" demands identifiable distinction; that is more than a cultural truth, it is an eternal truth. Christian conduct on earth must therefore match one's heavenly citizenship. It appears as though Paul did not sense a passionate conviction on their part to avoid assimilation into the people and culture around them. From the Pentecost experience (Acts 1–3)

---

[7] Acts 16:21
[8] Philippians 3:20

onward, the assimilation battle has always been a challenge for the people of God. Jean Baptiste Massillion (1663–1742) boldly and honestly reveals his personal struggle.

I fear that such around me may enfeeble me and seduce me into a crooked course of policy unworthy of thy glory.

I fear that insensibly I may become such a coward as to blush at thy name, such a sinner as to resist the impulses of thy grace, such a traitor as to withhold my testimony against sin, such a self-deceiver as to disguise my criminal timidity by the name of prudence.

Already I feel that this poison is insinuating itself into my heart, for while I would not have my conduct resemble that of the wicked who surround me, yet I am too much biased by the fear of giving them offense.

I dare not imitate them, but I'm almost as much afraid of irritating them.

I know that it is impossible both to please a corrupt world and a holy God, and yet I so far lose sight of this truth, that instead of sustaining me in decision, it only serves to render my vacillation the more inexcusable.

What remains for me but to implore thy help!

Strengthen me, O Lord, against these declensions so injurious to thy glory, so fatal to the fidelity which is due to thee. Cause me to hear thy strengthening and encouraging voice.

If the voice of thy grace be not lifted up in my spirit, re-animating my feeble faith, I feel that there is but a step between me and despair.

I am on the brink of the precipice, I am ready to fall into a criminal complicity with those who would fain drag me down with them into the pit.

A Different View: Opposition and Affliction

The very heartbeat of Paul's epistle is to enable the believers at Philippi to have no doubts about what it really means to be a slave or saint of Christ, what it really means to be different, and how a Christocentric life should be seen by people around them. He does *not* address peripheral issues like how they should dress, etc. His first task is to change their perspective of opposition and affliction, even about his own imprisonment (1:12–14). Writing to his friends *from prison*, he plainly models for them the difference he espouses: rather than his chains *hindering* the gospel, Paul declares they had been used to *advance* the gospel. Prison didn't close the door to his ministry or prevent the gospel from going forward. Prison actually opened new doors;

incarceration gave opportunities that could not have come otherwise.

That is a kingdom view of opposition and affliction; *that* is how a citizen of heaven should see trouble on earth; *that* is also different from their dominant culture. And *that* is also different from our own twenty-first-century approach to problems, opposition, and difficulties that we perceive as a hindrance to our progress. Our definition and identification of restraint obviously differ from the apostle's. We have myopically removed from our teaching the possibility that God may actually be using that very obstacle for His glory and purpose. Caution should be the catchword as we pray for God to remove painful things.

The Greek word the apostle uses for advance (1:12) is *pro-kope*; this is the word that is specially used for the progress of an army or expedition and is the noun form of the verb meaning *to cut down in advance*. Rather than seeing his imprisonment as an obstacle for God to remove, the apostle sees shackles and chains as a strategic military move for the army of heaven, sending Paul *to cut down in advance* obstacles on behalf of others who would follow with the gospel.

Luke records Paul's imprisonment was assigned to the Praetorian Guard, and Luke specifically names the leader who took Paul as prisoner to Rome: Julian (Acts 27). What natural eyes see as pain or prison, God sees as strategic placement. Paul's words certainly bear a different perspective of trouble, as opposed to the more common view, from which the Philippi believers would have asked God to remove the pain and oppression. As is our common prayer: take it away.

Thus Paul speaks as a true *doulos* (1:1), a slave with no will of his own, but one who willingly and joyfully accepts that his life is controlled by his Master. The life that is distinctively different in the face of opposition and affliction is what Paul wishes for the church at Philippi to understand and willingly embrace.

A Different Model: Humility over Position
The call for distinctive difference in the lives of the Philippians comes from Paul's heart; his thoughts are not particularly systematic, structured, or organized. They are more mosaic patterns of truth where no clear-cut lines complete and finish the picture. Interwoven in his tapestry are subtle rebukes against self-centeredness that has brought some measure of discord into the church family and threatens their unity.

No part of his gentle chastening is more vibrant than when he directs them to behold the correct model of humility, which can be found only in their King (2:3–8). Paul's thoughts are profound and radical, and he tells them they need a complete overhaul of their present mind-set in order to cure the infectious discord that they now experience. *His primary concern in these verses is to illustrate the kind of selflessness that is to make them different.*

Paul's use of words is deliberate *and* theological; *the links in his chain of thought are intense* in 2:6–7:

- "Being in the form of God..." This Greek word is *morphe*, which is the essential form of something *that never changes and is retained as long as the individual exists.* This is to say that Jesus is unalterably God. Eternally, His essence and His unchangeable being are divine.
- "Did not count equality with God as something to be *grasped*..." This Greek word is *harpagmos*, something clutched tightly, refusing to let it go, as a prize won.
- "But made himself *nothing*..." The Greek word is *kenoo*, which means to empty or pour out (literally) or to give up status and privilege (metaphorically). Paul is not saying Christ gave up any of His divine attributes (see *morphe*) but to show that Christ gave up the privileges and status that were rightfully his as God.
- "Taking the *form* of a *servant*..." The same Greek words were previously used *morphe* (essence) and *doulos* (bond slave). What Paul means is that when Jesus became man, it was not play-acting; it was reality. He was really and truly man.

In vivid terms Paul makes these verses about Christ's humility, the basic imperative of the entire epistle. Without doubt, Paul's appeal is for them to actively think like Christ thought, to *actively* apply his model to their personal Christian experience, not just to have a passive opinion of assent to the rightness of his theology.

Transcultural: Eternal Unchanging Truth

It would not be amiss to suggest that Paul's encouragement for his friends to be distinctively different was to serve as a reminder of kingdom truth, which living in Philippi had jaded. His expectation of them was not to be left open for misinterpretation. What did he expect from them? He made it clear.

- He expected them to stand fast-firm in their identity as slaves and saints of the living God, willfully and joyfully embracing the surrender of all their rights to God.
- He expected them to have an attitude of being unconquerable by the culture of Rome; they were to live as citizens of heaven assigned to a worldly outpost while living out heaven's rule.
- He expected them to live with courage and honor (even joy) in the face of opposition and affliction.
- He expected them to be exemplary and unwavering when their commitment was pushed to the limits, to follow the model of their own elder, Epaphraditus.

- He expected them to change their minds about their own self-importance, stand in unshakable unity, and discover kingdom humility, which had been patterned for them by their King.

Paul's consummate charge was this: your whole life, word, and behavior are to be lived in a manner that brings no embarrassment to the King you represent. Walk worthy of the message you declare; walk worthy of the King you cherish. The apostle's own motivation was wrapped tightly in a sense of courage and honor. *"Regardless of what happens to me, let me so live, or so die, that Christ is honored."*[9]

How do we transfer the eternal truth of this epistle so we may live as citizens of heaven in the here and now of the twenty-first century? If we are to minimize assimilation into our dominant culture, what do we focus on? How do we have kingdom impact on the topsy-turvy world around us?

1. We need to take definitive and proactive steps to possess the mind of Christ and make it our new mind-set.
2. The evidence and demonstration of that new mind should be seen as we refrain from egotistical pursuits and rather become bond slaves to serving God and man. We should be less "self" oriented.
3. We must become models of humility that all men can see.

---

[9] Philippians 1:20

4. Our motives should be carefully examined.
5. We should live obediently before God regardless of the personal cost.
6. We follow the example of Christ to put others first, even at the cost of personal gain and ambition.
7. We must trust that God keeps good records! He sees... He knows...and He does not forget.
8. We leave both vindication and exaltation to God.

The Christ pattern of citizenship would seem quite foreign to Roman citizenship or any other earthly society they knew about. *But it was to become the norm for all believers of all cultures of all generations.*

The countercultural theme the apostle presents as normal kingdom living is made even more startling when we remember where Paul was sitting when he wrote. Sitting bound by chains in a terrible Roman prison, the freedom of his spirit could not be constrained. So great was the revelation of Christ in him, his vocabulary was hardly able to find human expression for that which was immeasurable, for a life in Christ that prisons and chains could not imprison, for revelation that flowed from the deep secrets of the eternal God.

Paul speaks of the exalted Christ, sitting at the right hand of God. He speaks of Christ being the center of all things, God's agent to reconcile all things as God intended, the invading work of the Holy Spirit as the enabling indweller of the believer's soul, revealing how God's ways provide the only wise and worthy way for the redeemed to live.

Assimilation is not an option.

"We must get to know God in secret—alone in the desert. It does seem to me that true spirituality lies in this—utter dependence on God for everything. We shall dread to do anything in our own wisdom. If a man can only get down before God and get His plan of work for him, that is what will make him irresistible. It does not matter whether he is a strong man or a weak one."

Hudson Taylor
It is Not Death to Die!

· 4 ·

The Culture of God's Kingdom

The past generation of American believers has adopted a convoluted form of divine grace that is so inclusive that transformed living is neither expected nor seen as essential to Christ-likeness. It seems that discipleship and trans-formation have become optional to the Christian journey as believers assimilate into this new societal-shaped Christian culture...just ask God to forgive your sin and all is well. However, there is inherent miscalculation in just repeating "the sinner's prayer."

From the beginning of His public ministry, Jesus had one thematic message: the kingdom of God. It can be broken down into three parts:

- How do you enter the kingdom?
- How do you live once in the kingdom?
- What does life look like in the kingdom?

Entrance into the Kingdom

The thematic message of Jesus, a new kingdom and a new King, is the quintessential discipline of divine rule and requires a radical departure from the old kingdom of self-rule. It becomes life on God's terms, not mine. The transfer of my right to rule to God is the fly in the ointment for most living in America's egalitarian democratic culture; many still resist the idea of yielding their intrinsic my-life-on-my-terms mind-set.

The yearning of God's heart is not to be exclusionary, but it is purposely intentionally separating. He provides the opportunity for all to enter His kingdom, but it will be on His terms. God's redemptive plan of forgiveness, reconciliation, and restored relationship unalterably passes through the divine person Jesus Christ; He is the only entrance into kingdom culture.

The key to redemption is not *primarily* a sinner's prayer, or even asking forgiveness of sin, but rather embracing the kingdom of God (the rule of God) and the lordship of Jesus. That is, *redemption is the reversal of authority and rule in one's life.* Paul said in Romans that to be "saved" a person must openly declare that Jesus is Lord and believe in his or her heart that God has raised Him from the dead. Redemption then follows. "If you confess with your mouth that Jesus is Lord and believe in your heart that God raised him from the dead, *you will be saved.* For with the heart one believes and is justified, and with the mouth one confesses and *is saved.*"[1]

---

[1]Romans 1:9–10

The beginning point of kingdom life is *a transfer of rule*. He is the Lord—not me, not you, not society's persuasive culture. The first step in my redemption is to dethrone one ruler and enthrone a new ruler over my life. God's culture of life is not our natural preference. It is a radical and extraordinary choice, a choice not everyone can make. Every generation has had multitudes who want the benefits of the King and His kingdom, but who are unwilling to embrace the fact that as sovereign Lord He mandates life in His kingdom be lived in harmony with His nature and character.

The missing piece to our present-day all-inclusive culture is failure to abandon a lifestyle that is contrary to God's nature: holiness. When Jesus spoke to the woman caught in the act of adultery, He was forgiving but also *requiring*. Our dominant culture loves to use one short phrase Jesus spoke during this encounter: "neither do I condemn you." However, to take note of only one part of His conversation, the words of forgiveness, is misguided in its humanly inspired attempts to allow everyone into the kingdom. Their all-inclusive form of love is inadequate to produce a changed life. To omit Jesus' "go and sin no more" requirement, or "stop doing what you have been doing," is failure to grasp His broader intentionality: begin a new way of living...free, yet reordered.[2]

---

[2] The full account is found in John 8:1–11.

Willingness to accept the lordship of Jesus is the gateway that allows me entrance into the kingdom of God. Everything else Jesus taught is a description of how life is to be lived once *in* the kingdom, including dealing with sin. Accepting by faith the new kingdom nature rule of God, with both its grace and requirements, provides for me a security that is independent of my efforts; thus by him alone my eternal life has been attained.

Works do not become soteriological but vocational. What I do does not produce my salvation; how I live springs from my salvation. Once in the kingdom by accepting divine rule, I now must learn how to live as a viable citizen within a new culture. Thus, a lifelong process must be embraced, a lifelong commitment to grow into Christ-likeness; there *must be a legitimate effort* to emulate the model that Jesus came to demonstrate.

Life in the Kingdom

One of the most insightful teaching sessions in the life of Jesus takes place on a mountainside, not in a worship center, like the temple in Jerusalem. The Sermon on the Mount is a brief manual for living out a distinctive counterculture experience once inside the kingdom (Matt. 5–7).

Starting with the Beatitudes, the word *blessed* sets the tone for the whole sermon. In verses 3–11, Jesus' context for the word *blessed* reflects a state of well-being while in covenant relationship with God. Whether one is poor, mourning, seeking righteousness, or developing a pure heart, or even while being persecuted, insulted, or falsely accused, God still reigns. Jesus then presents these pragmatic identifiers of life in the kingdom:

- the criteria of being "different" (salt and light) (5:13)
- practicing kingdom principles, not earthly principles (17)
- dealing with anger, not venting and excusing your outburst (21)
- being morally pure in marriage, not justifying uncontrolled urges (27)
- divorce (31)
- keeping your word simple: yes means yes and no means no (33)
- do not seek revenge; rather than plotting it, let it go (38)
- love your enemies rather than yielding to hatred (43)
- give to the needy without drawing attention to yourself (6:1)
- prayer joins me with the fatherhood of God without drawing attention to self (5–13)
- having proper motivation in fasting without drawing attention to yourself (16–18)
- the vulnerability of earthly treasures (19–21)
- multiple warnings against worry; rather, trust God (25)
- don't judge others; focus on fixing your own faults and short-comings (7:1)
- trust in the verity of God when He says, "Ask me!" (7)

This message demonstrates how lifestyle in God's kingdom culture is the way to affirm a genuine alternative manner of being human and spiritually reborn at the same time. God's ways and God's precepts expose conventional culture as not only inadequate but profoundly eschatologically myopic; the dominant culture simply makes provision for the here and now.

Jesus ties these various teachings on kingdom dynamics together with the conjunctive *"Therefore* I tell you..." There is a distinct common thread woven through the first twenty-four verses in this chapter: man's perceived need for things to secure his life and his future. Father God's answer to man is *not* to give him revelation of some previously hidden mystery so that he can now lay hold of the goods that will secure his future. *His answer is for man to* **redefine life**.

Explaining what a redefined life is like once you are in the kingdom, Jesus gives His listeners a simple directive: "Therefore I tell you, do not be anxious about your *life*, what you will eat, or what you will drink; nor about your body, what you will put on. *Is not* **life** *more than food; and the body more than clothing?*" (6:25). This is possibly the most powerful question in the NT.

But I want to modify the question rather slightly so it becomes personal:

"Isn't *your* life more than…?"
"Isn't your *life* more than…?"
"Isn't your life *more than*…?"

The Greek word used for life two times in this verse is *psuche*,[3] meaning heart, soul, mind, and the essence of personality and being. Jesus is directing the attention of these people away from a focus of life that has been merely on being physically alive and having the basic ingredients that sustain longevity and duration. He redefines life from the new kingdom perspective with a focus on the qualities and purposes that give *life to the essence of who you are*.

The dominant culture of most generations defines for them a life that is held together by acquisition and consumption. Societal norms even enhance a very stubborn defensive posture supporting the acquisition approach to life. A very wealthy young man once asked Jesus what he needed to do to inherit eternal life. When he heard the answer, he turned away deeply disappointed. He could not bring himself to relinquish his acquisitional and consumptive lifestyle by giving everything to the poor.[4]

---

[3] Other examples of psuche are found in: Matthew 2:20—sought the child's *life*; Matthew 20:28—gives his *life* a ransom for many; John 10:11–17—lay down his *life* for the sheep.
[4] Mark 10:17–31

Listen to Jesus expound the difference between just being alive and having real value in *being alive*!

- The birds don't build barns to store up for tomorrow, but the Father feeds them. "Are ye not much more valuable than they?" (6:26).
- The lilies don't labor but are better adornment for God's fields than Solomon and all his wealth and gaudy jewelry. "Will He not much more clothe you, O you of little faith?" (6:28–31).

In order to live vibrantly and with significant meaning, we must understand what precept should be most important to anyone choosing to live by kingdom principles: the eternal must invade the temporal. Jesus made the point quite clear, "For after all these things do the Gentiles seek: for your heavenly Father knows that you have need of all these things" (32). The term *Gentiles* is used to represent all peoples living outside a covenant relationship with God. Thus, the message of Jesus is that people in covenant relationship with God seek different things in life. They have different priorities.

The counsel and caution of Jesus is this: *don't reduce your life down to the basics...isn't the essence of your being* **more than** *the very basic elements of things and quantities?* Your *life*! Yet how much time is disproportionately spent on these very things? Start to take notice of how much time you spend thinking/praying/reminding God about the resources you need for today's household issues: house payments, car payments, dental bills, electric bills, gas bills, a broken lawn-mower, leaking faucets, noisy washing machines, an a/c that doesn't cool well, worn and stained carpets, an old roof, insurance payments, the kids' clothes.

Add to that the amount of time spent thinking/praying/ reminding God about tomorrow's issues: college for the kids, your aging neighborhood, your aging body, retirement, your 401K return, IRAs, paying off the mortgage, staying healthy so you can enjoy retiring, etc. What becomes clear is that the majority of our prayers are spent in trying to get God to make problems go away.

The Lord of the universe *knows*. The issue is for *you* to know a greater truth about His kingdom...your *life* ought not be reduced to or dominated by the lowest common denomi-nator (i.e., your personal well-being). His counter-cultural message is to leave your well-being in the hands of the God with whom you have a covenant. In Jesus' redefined king-dom life, *the greater truth* is not necessarily for us to let go of asking for divine intervention regarding these things but to grow to a place so as not to become crisis oriented. *Today's need is not to eclipse tomorrow's purpose!*

In redefining life from the kingdom view, *that* is what Jesus is saying! Isn't your *life* more than:

- what you will eat
- what you will wear
- the size of your house
- the age of your car

One of the difficulties the people of God have had in recent years is tenaciously clinging to the idea that one of God's primary objectives is to assure they reach personal happiness and satisfaction by acquiring plenty of "stuff." But the growing saint soon discovers that satisfaction, as so defined, is as elusive as the pot of gold at the rainbow's end.

God is ever nudging us onward beyond the basics of life and living—into the *more than*. We should always be thankful for everything God has done for us, thankful that as the Psalmist said, "Your carts overflow with abundance..."[5] (i.e., wherever God goes, good things just happen). But we must learn not to *resist* the ways God chooses to lead us into "more." Not more "stuff," not more "things"...but into more *life*.

Occasionally I will pick up my copy of Victor Frankl's classic *Man's Search for Meaning* and re-read it. The first half of the book reflects on the three years he spent in the death camps of Auschwitz and Dachau during World War II. Those pages are far more than merely recounting an historical event,

---

[5] Psalm 65:11

even more than horrible stories of what one human being can do to another…they are pages filled with spiritual truth.

The great penetrating thought in Frankl's book is this: people who have something to live for, a vision, a dream, a hope, a person, or *something significant in their life* **not yet finished** were the more likely to survive. Frankl concluded, "The prisoner who had lost faith in the future, his future, was doomed."[6]

Doesn't that sound a lot like the message Jesus was declaring in Matthew 6? If your life is so intertwined with your "stuff" that your "stuff" is the defining of who you are, you might want to stop and see if you are really in the kingdom or not! If you lose your "stuff," will the essence of who and what you are diminish? Only if the essence of your life is measured by the myopic definitions of what is important as determined by the dominant culture: the restaurants you frequent; the sticker price on your car; the designer name on your shirt.

So, is the very essence of your being (your life), as designed by the Creator, to reach its apex of fulfillment with *things*? Absolutely not! Listen carefully to what Jesus said: "A man's life *(zoe) does not* consist in the abundance of his

---

[6] Victor Frankl, Man's Search For Meaning. (New York: Washington Square Press, 1984), 95.

possessions" (Luke 12:15). The falsehood of the dominant culture cannot be made more obvious!

In John 10:10 Jesus said, "I am come that they might have life and have it more abundantly." Guess what? He doesn't define this abundant life He came to impart as something equated with tangible *stuff*. It has to do with transforming the essence of your *being*. It has to do with bringing God's full and complete life into you so you have a full and complete *life*. It is imparted so you can walk in the fullness of God's purpose for you—a purpose worthy of your *life*.

I want to rephrase this: to live in God's culture you must prepare yourself to think, plan, act, speak, and pray with a kingdom perspective that is worthy of your *life*. Learn to see today's interests in the scheme of God's eternal purposes. Focus on what Jesus focused on in Matthew 5–7. Emphasize what Jesus emphasized in Matthew 5–7.

Consequences of Cultural Assimilation

Now we come to the challenging, and to many, disturbing "broad way-narrow way" and the "many-few" teaching that wraps up this profound teaching of being spiritually reborn into God's new culture. "Enter through the narrow gate. For wide is the gate and broad is the road that leads to destruction, and many enter through it. But small is the gate and narrow the road that leads to life; and only a few find it."[7]

Jesus makes it clear that *every person* will *consciously* assimilate into *some culture*, either the dominant culture of his or her society or the distinctive counterculture of the kingdom of God. No other options are available.

Moving from the dominant broad way to a radical narrow way is not easy; most never make the move. The broad way is the path of least resistance, which most people follow: self-indulgence, limited boundaries, the pursuit of attention, revenge, hatred, etc., which leads to destruction and loss in life. The narrow way is to live by kingdom principles: submission to God's ways, blessing those who do not deserve to be blessed, trusting God in the face of evidence that is contrary, etc., which leads to a life that is lived in a state of well-being (blessed) in relationship with God.

The ever-popular self-help books of the past generation have not helped Christians figure out kingdom living and culture at all. The common denominator of most Christian self-help books is to massively exaggerate one's own capabilities. The real truth is that self-will and self-sufficiency rely on a failed strategy traceable back to Eden. They rely on *my* ability to shape, mold, and control *my* life and on *my*

---

[7] Matthew 7:13–14

logic and reasoning to know what is good or bad for *my* life. That is the centricity of the broad way that leads to destruction and loss.

At this point, let me open to you a daring conclusion in juxtaposition to traditional interpretations of these two verses. Common theologies make a dramatic and sudden shift from Jesus' how-life-is-lived in the kingdom of God into a soteriological and eschatological meaning. Traditional theology declares that all of a sudden Jesus is saying many take the easy way and go to destruction-hell, while only a few take the narrow way and enter eternal life-heaven. Re-read this passage from a life-in-the-kingdom view.

We need to look *carefully* at two words in these verses: destruction and life.

1. Destruction (*apoleia*: ruin, waste, loss—can be physical, emotional, spiritual) as used in verse 13, destruction is to be found along the broad way. But *apoleia* has no NT connection to eternal damnation-destruction, which is an entirely different word (*kresis*: a decision or judgment from a tribunal for punishment, damnation or penal infliction). *Kresis* is used in Matthew 23:14, Mark 3:20, John 5:29, and other NT verses that *do speak* directly to eternal judgment, eternal death, fiery judgment, punishment, hell fire, destruction, etc.

2. Life (*zoe*: to live, have vitality, be quickened—have life in the absolute sense, whether applied to a plant, a pet, a person, or even to God Himself) as used in verse 14 is to have *real, vibrant life* while being alive! This kind of life is found in the narrow way that few find—by self-surrender to God's ways of living.

These two verses are the *conclusion*, the *summary*, of all that Jesus has said in his message on life in the kingdom of God and its culture. They are *neither* soteriological nor eschatological; they speak *neither* to one's salvation nor to one's eternal destiny. They do speak directly to the fullness of life or emptiness of life one *willfully chooses in this present life*.

A paraphrasing would be like this, "In conclusion, life in the kingdom of God is available to all, but not many are willing to let go of self-rule and self-determinism. It is hard to die to oneself, but if you do not, it will ultimately lead to a life marred by pain, loss, injury, and even destruction. Unfortunately, most people will take the easy way of life and cling to their self-rule and self-indulgence. However, if you will make the choice to walk in the narrow way and embrace the ways of God, even though your flesh will resist, you will discover what real living is all about...being free, being whole, being vibrant, and being genuine!"

Herein is the tension for entrance into the kingdom: there is enough reality in the broad way for it to seem viable, but it is an illusion soon leading to disappointment, injury, even severe losses in one's life. The narrowness of kingdom culture may also be seen as illusory, but in the exact opposite manner; narrowness proves to be anything but narrow. Its ultimate reality is not confining, but rather it leads to the openness of freedom, peace, and authentic contentment... *and real life with God.*

The narrow way, choosing to surrender to God's rule and ways, is the way that leads to real life, which offers real hope, real peace, and real security—the very things my grasping, clinging, self-empowered living annuls.

- My hope can only be found in the name of what is holy, not in what is common.
- My security will be found in the name of what is born of the Spirit, not of the flesh.
- My life can only be found in surrender, not in acquisition.

Assimilating into the kingdom of God and its distinctively different culture, which adds life to living, requires a unique death experience...death to "self." That alone makes it far too narrow and restrictive to many people. It is quite foreign to contemporary "self" thinking that letting go of anything (death) my "self" likes can actually be for my good and produce meaningful life. But that is exactly what Jesus taught in the whole of His ministry. His strongest requirement of disciples is this: "Whoever wants to be my disciple must deny themselves and take up their cross and follow me."[8]

His other-world-first and other-person-first life proposal has the requirement of death: to self-determinism, self-awareness, self-indulgence, and self-rule. The word *deny* (*aparneomai*: to disown, repudiate, deny) is the linchpin to it all. To deny oneself means to personally undo the deception done in Eden by the Serpent: "Your eyes will be opened, and you will be like God, knowing good and evil."[9] It means to disown and repudiate my "self" as the dominant decision maker of life, it means to recognize I do not really know what is right and wrong for my life, it means to dethrone "self" and enthrone God as the ruling and dominant source of my life.

The gospel writers Matthew, Mark, and Luke all record the plain, often difficult, mandate of Jesus that in order to follow him a person must disavow and abstain from "self" and assimilate into God's radical culture. Taking up the cross of self-denial prohibits assimilation into the present acquisitional and consumptive culture, while at the same time energizing assimilation into God's eternal culture *here* in a temporal setting.

Taking up this unique cross proves not to be death but ultimate life—the life few find.

---

[8]Matthew 16:24, Mark 8:34, Luke 9:23
[9]Genesis 3:5

"Why do humans naturally resist God's moral order? Because behind all the arguments is a clenched fist. Behind all the intellectual verbiage is a covert desire to have a world without God."

Ravi Zacharias
The End of Reason

· 5 ·

Philosophy and Ethics

A powerful politician once asked, "What is truth?" Whether Pilate's question[1] was meant to be rhetorical, contemptuous, or philosophical, he captured in three simple words the very foundation of how life is structured. If truth and falsehood are the scales upon which life is measured, this necessitates some real soul searching: *What* do you believe? *Why* do you believe it? *How* do you know it's true? *Who* told you it was true? *Why* should you believe them?

The construction of one's philosophical and ethical foundation is no trivial matter. For the Christian, no instruction on how to build a solid Christian philosophical and ethical base is clearer than the guidelines given by the apostle Paul to the churches surrounding the Mediterranean, particularly the church in Colossae. I will address that passage shortly.

In simple (but accurate) terms, "philosophies and ethics" are more commonly referred to and understood by most people as "beliefs and values"—what you believe and what you value. Every person in every culture has a belief system and a value system; the challenge is to live so the two are equally

---

[1] John 18:38

interchangeable parts working in harmony. If they contradict each other, the result is hypocrisy—saying you believe one thing (your philosophy of life) while doing the exact opposite (your ethics of life).

What we value should be the same as what we believe. It should be. For followers of Christ, the closer these two become (beliefs and values), the stronger the moral commitment to real kingdom culture and to God's truth. If what I publicly profess as a Christian is not matched by what I do as a Christian, where is the problem? Each believer must stay on guard and be clearly focused so his or her Christian belief system (philosophy) is not just passionate sound and fury that is then undermined by an inconsistent lifestyle (ethics). If that happens, the result is hypocrisy… and I am not sure anything can be more damaging to a Christian's testimony in the public eye than to be seen as hypocritical.

Making the Two One

Here is a simple example of how the belief system and the value system can be differentiated. At the beginning of almost every college course I have taught, I asked the class how many of them believe cheating on an exam is wrong—100 percent raised their hands to say yes. My follow-up question shows the distinction between a belief system and a value system: "How many of you have cheated on an exam?" Almost everyone raised their hand again, indicating yes. Though their belief system (philosophy of life) is "being honest," their value system (ethics and practice) is quite clear: a higher grade supersedes honesty. "I believe in honesty, but I *really* need a high grade in this course; therefore I cheat."

For followers of Christ, all philosophies must ultimately be placed in contrast to the teaching and *person* of Jesus Christ. For such a disciple, it is more than just embracing life philosophies and ethics as abstract and theoretical but more clearly, embracing beliefs (philosophies) and values (ethics) based on the teaching of Christ and on how He modeled those in real living.

The Christo-centric belief system of Christianity has changed in the past generation to such a degree that there seems to be little relationship between this newly evolved belief system and biblical Christo-centric values. The newly adapted ideological belief system that began to be formed in the latter portion of the twentieth century and continues to evolve into the first two decades of the twenty-first century has begun descending the slippery slope of convenience and acceptability. It increasingly slides into an easy assimilation with worldly philosophies. This contrived convenience of trying to fit together two incongruent philosophies (light and darkness) threatens the necessity of Spirit-formed character and the distinctive message of salvation in Christ alone, both of which are required for biblical Christo-centric values.

The temptation is always there to make the gospel more popular, to individuals and to the general populace as well: 1) Surely it would be wise to make it easier for individuals to embrace the gospel by teaching its message in such a way that radical change is not necessary for people to become Christians. 2) Surely there will be broader acceptance of the gospel if people can see the gospel as a non-threatening non-demanding optional way of life and thought system that their own intellect can grasp, develop, and shape.

It is here at the point of unnatural and untenable blending of two systems of belief that the apostle Paul speaks a strong warning to the saints in Colossae. He is addressing a form of theology-philosophy that was aggressively attempting to infiltrate the church with an alternative worldview wrapped in the guise of higher knowledge. Paul identified two thought patterns in this intrusive teaching that actually *opposed* the gospel while trying to assimilate with the gospel: one was speculative, philosophical, and appealing to the intellect; the second was more practical and appealed to a stoical and ascetic lifestyle. But the common message in each train of thought was that *Christ was not enough*. You needed *this* for correct spiritual understanding.

Paul's warning is very clear: "See to it that no one takes you captive through hollow and deceptive philosophy, which depends on human tradition and the basic principles of this world rather than on Christ."[2] The word Paul used for "captive" (*sulagogein*) means to lead away as a prize of war and was often used to describe a slave trader carrying away people into bondage and slavery. Paul goes straight to the heart of the matter: mixing Christ (inclusively the person and his Word) with worldly wisdom and human tradition is eternally dangerous. The consequence of rejecting truth is becoming vulnerable to embracing a lie; the consequence of embracing a lie is bondage.

What Is Safe, What Is Dangerous

The primary distinction between what was dangerous to Paul's theology and what was safe for believers to embrace has to do with the source. In Paul's theology Christ was the centrality and full sufficiency of divine revelation for man. Living by Christ's precepts is the only safe place for a believer to be. What was considered dangerous theology-philosophy by Paul was based on human tradition and the basic principles of this world, which were *added* to knowledge of Christ, as if that divine knowledge was inadequate in and of itself. Generations later the differences between Christ-revealed theology and human traditions are just as real. Why wouldn't they be? Theological light and philosophical darkness *still* have no commonality.

Assimilating the simplicity of a faith-oriented gospel into a philosophy posing as intellectual exclusivity (*"Wow! That is*

---

[2] Colossians 2:8

really deep!") is nothing more than a feeble attempt to make the good news attractive to the pseudo-mystic. In other words, from the view of this threatening philosophy, a simple belief system based on the church's historical teaching of Christ is not enough to provide one with real, true spiritual meaning and salvation; only those who embrace the mystically and intellectually titillating can *really know* the truth of God.

However, what sounds good to the intellect may in fact be life threatening to the soul. When steps are taken to modify the gospel with hollow and empty philosophies not based on Christ, it is always the purity of truth that is diluted. Worldly philosophies are always elevated by the inclusion of Christian principles, but biblical transformational truth becomes weakened and degraded when adjoined to the world's values and to human traditions.

That is Paul's warning.

The Snare of Sophia
Are we to avoid all forms of philosophy? Certainly not. In its most simple and abbreviated description, the Greek word *philosophia* is the compound expression *philo* (love) -*sophia* (wisdom)…the love of wisdom. It is this benign definition we use in referencing a philosophy of business, a philosophy of marriage, work, war, racism, politics, and education, *ad infinitum*. But Paul had much more eternal things in mind.

In its more comprehensive description in the Pauline era, the love of wisdom was rooted in the recognition and worship of the goddess Sophia, thus becoming *"philo-sophia,"* the love of Sophia and what she stands for. So the love of wisdom in Paul's warning is more rightly a warning about a *love for the precepts represented by the goddess Sophia*, or, the adoration and love of Sophia herself. What did Sophia bring to the conversation? Sophia is a cosmic figure, an eternal spirit, who reveals *a spiritual worship of the universe, the cosmos*. Therefore, she offers the wisdom of man at the suppression of the wisdom of God to those who long to be spiritual apart from divine revelation.

Sophia, when found in the teachings of modern-day Christian mysticism, is a spirit thought to be expressed in all creation and the entire natural world—that is, *the divine is all things, and all thing are divine*. Whether aware or not, people drawn to the philosophy that God is only really found in the blending of matter and spirit are indeed accepting a version of ancient astrology and pantheism mixed with New Age universalism.

This source of ancient wisdom was supposed to lead a person to knowledge of the divine, resulting in the actualization of the divine into one's humanity through personal transformation found in one's *"self."* Or God is already in you; when you really find your true *"self,"* you will find God. In the Gnostic theology-philosophy, which the apostles were constantly combating as it infiltrated the church, the Gnostics adapted this ancient Sophia spirit into their theology as an intellectual pathway to the deep things of God. How unlike the principles of Christ's kingdom. The kingdom's ethics are defined by God Himself and are actualized only by redemption. While the unregenerate find God's moral requirements foolish and unnecessary, the regenerated find them protecting, if not even comforting.

The puzzling thing is how people who have been redeemed and brought into God's freedom and liberty could ever contemplate opening themselves to any teaching that is contradictory to the plain truth of Scripture. The most common targets for rejection by vain philosophies are the diety of Christ and the authenticity of Scripture as the revealed Word of God. Because they so easily argue away the God of the Bible and do not accept that Christ is the revelation of that God, the very core of Christendom is vacated. In Paul's time, in order to attract believers, the lovers of Sophia had to bring something to the discussion; some replacement had to be made viable and acceptable. So they elevated man's place in the scheme of time and eternity; they maximized human intellect while minimizing divine revelation.

Writing to the people being tempted by this intellectually appealing dogma of Jesus *plus something*, or Christ *plus something*, Paul makes very clear that nothing more is needed than Christ. No wisdom or understanding was superior to Jesus Christ; He alone was their sufficiency. In Colossians 1:15–20, no less than seven times Paul uses the word *all* to describe the majesty and magnitude of Christ's person and work:

- Christ is the visible image of the invisible God, and He is over *all creation (everything)*
- He created *all things* in heaven and on earth, visible and invisible, all thrones, powers, rulers, and authorities *(everything)*
- *All things* were created by Him and for Him *(everything)*
- He was before *all things (everything)*
- He holds *all things* together *(everything)*
- *All* the fullness of God dwells in Him *(every aspect of character and diety)*
- *All things* are reconciled to God by making peace through Christ's blood, shed on the cross *(everything)*

There are no limitations in Christ. *"In everything he has the supremacy"* (v.18). The cross-cultural pollination of NT Christ theology with the vain, hollow philosophies of human tradition results in a defective and impotent form of hybrid religion, regardless of how intellectually appealing it may appear. The work of the Holy Spirit is not to make us blend into the current philosophical and ethical mind-set. Rather, His great work is conforming us to the image of God's Son.[3] At what point do we as Christ followers come to grips with the utter necessity that non-conformity and separation from the world's philosophies and values are not an option?

In Christ

In Pauline theology, two words permeate the entirety of his teaching: "in Christ." Over 133 times he uses this phrase to describe the fullness of God's redemptive plan, which works for God's glory and man's good. It is obvious the *Christ plus something* needed for pseudo-super-religious intelligence falls far short of the unsearchable wisdom of the eternal God. Look carefully at these samples of Paul's exposure of vain philosophies and the revelation of Christ's completeness:

- the *righteousness* of God is found *in Christ* (Rom. 3:22)
- *eternal life* is found *in Christ* (Rom. 6:23)
- the *Spirit of life* is found *in Christ* (Rom. 8:2)
- the *love of God* is found *in Christ* (Rom. 8:39)
- the *grace of God* is found *in Christ* (1 Cor. 1:4)
- we are *made free men in Christ* (1 Cor. 7:22)
- *God established us in Christ* (2 Cor. 1:21)
- *God leads us to triumph in Christ* (2 Cor. 2:14)
- we are *justified before God in Christ* (Gal. 2:16)
- we are *made sons of God in Christ* (Gal. 3:26)
- *God's eternal purposes* are set *in Christ* (Eph. 1:9)
- *the riches of God's grace* are found *in Christ* (Eph. 2:7)
- *salvation* is *in Christ* (Eph. 2:13)

---

[3] Romans 8:29

- *God's promises* are *in Christ* (Eph. 3:6)
- the *truth* is *in Christ* (Eph. 4:27)
- the *light* is *in Christ* (Eph. 5:8)
- our *righteousness* is *in Christ* (Phil. 3:9)
- *God supplies our needs in Christ* (Phil. 4:19)
- *spiritual maturity* is found *in Christ* (Col. 1:18)
- *our confidence* is *in Christ* (2 Thess. 3:4)
- *faith and love* are *in Christ* (1 Tim. 1:14)
- *life* is *in Christ* (2 Tim. 1:1)

Paul's approach is quite simple: he sets worldly wisdom-philosophy against the higher wisdom of God the Creator. And earthly wisdom fails. Every generation needs to think about its conception and view of God and make the same comparison Paul made. Is the comparison made by each generation true to God's self-revelation in Scripture, or is it being guided by energized humanistic thought? Particularly each generation must look at the picture of Jesus' life as He portrays, "God among us,"[4] as "God come in the flesh,"[5] and as he declared to Phillip, "If you have seen me, you have seen the Father."[6] Christ is the consummate end of God's redemptive history; He is the end of the law for all who believe; He is the end of all self-effort and striving. God has made Christ to be our wisdom, our righteousness, our sanc-

---

[4] Matthew 1:23, John 1:14
[5] 1 Timothy 3:16
[6] John 14:9–10

tification, and our redemption.[7] How does hollow philosophy compare to that?

The inherent danger of first-century Gnosticism and its present-day resurgence rests in its chameleon-like characteristics and subtle nuances. Its religious-ethical-moral-philosophical system could/can easily hide within the dogmas of almost any religion. Hiding cannot be done by loudly proclaiming its deception but by a quiet assimilation of *some* truth mixed with *some* error folded into biblical doctrine. When taken into the shadowy and peripheral teaching of the "mysterious," the appeal to human logic and reasoning becomes extraordinary. It appeals to the mind in ways that subtly invalidate the gospel of Christ. Consequently, biblical Christianity often finds itself in direct confrontation with present-day moral attitudes and philosophies in defining truth.

The Philosophical Dismantling of Christianity

This short list captures the essence of the core ideals of humanistic conclusions and philosophies that are experiencing a renewed focus toward dismantling traditional Christianity. This is the hollow philosophy about which Paul warned. It:

- redefines biblical truth and doctrine through the lens of philosophy and human reasoning.

---

[7]1 Corinthians 1:30

- challenges the reality of *revelation* as a viable source of truth (i.e., denial of the inspiration of Scripture).
- challenges the viability of any concept of divine intervention in normal life (e.g., miracles).
- creates an unresolvable tension between faith and reason, almost to the complete exclusion of faith.
- makes biblical understanding a "completely objective" experience with no room for the "subjective."
- marginalizes Scripture as a unique expression of the sovereign God (i.e., making the Bible an ordinary history book).
- redefines Christ as *not* the hypostatic union of God come in the flesh, Jesus, but as the confluence of the material world and the spirit world, therefore making all things divine.

Unfortunately, the influence of this form of theology-philosophy continues to grow well into the twenty-first century and probably will continue to expand as long as men search for ways to minimize subjection to a real and living God while emphasizing their own importance. Whether openly rejecting God's truth or willingly suppressing the truth, both plainly mean a person is willing to live life with inferior substitutes...and with their eternal consequences.

The revelation that came to the psalmist is worth noting: "Your decrees are very trustworthy."[8] God only speaks truth. To do otherwise would contradict and destroy His holy character; therefore, what He declares can be trusted. The question is simple: Which shall we trust—the wisdom of men or the wisdom of God?

[8] Psalm 93:5

"**The whole history of the world is discovered to be but a contest between the wisdom of God and the cunning of Satan.**"

A.W. Tozer
The Knowledge of the Holy

· 6 ·

The Influence of Culture, Social Theology, and Gender on Biblical Interpretation

The texts of Scripture obviously have a specific truth or principle relative to the people to whom they were written; our present-day objective is to determine the timeless and eternal truth of God *within* the text. As an eternal truth, God's Word must speak to all generations. If it does not, it has little relevance for any generation; this necessitates that the primary principle *not be* culturally bound. It must be relevant to both the original hearers *and* to a contemporary audience as well. Reading Scripture from a twenty-first-century per-spective means I must find and apply the eternal principles of God's word *without* trying to seek and forcefully apply the original cultural detail of its context.

The Bible is a book about real-life people with real-life needs; the background data (historical-cultural context)[1] adds emo-tion and intensity to how God related to those people. Because there is eternal truth contained in the historical-cultural truth, the life stories found in these biblical biogra-

---

[1] Historical-cultural context is the social, religious, political, and economic information relevant to the time of the writing. Even geography may tie together pertinent details with additional insights to the truth.

phies will provide people in *every* generation from *every* culture a picture of how *all* people can expect God to relate to them in *their* culture.

What do we, hundreds of years removed from scriptural writing, bring to the historical-cultural context? Is that important? Absolutely. All of us are unavoidably influenced by our culture; it is so deeply engrained into who and what we are that it is impossible to remain completely objective when approaching biblical interpretation and application. We tend to fill any gaps in our understanding of biblical meaning, or "how" we are going to apply biblical principles, *with our culture.* Nothing makes this clearer than the dynamics of *presuppositions* or *preunderstanding.*

These two terms simply mean it is impossible to ignore everything that has made you who you are. All of your life experiences, parental input, former teachers, books that have impacted you, friends who have blessed you, enemies who have hurt you, joys, ups-and-downs, etc., have both consciously and subconsciously influenced how you think and interpret life.

In fact, presuppositions represent what a person *considers to be the truth* about any subject until additional evidence, or input, changes his or her thinking. Presuppositions are not automatically wrong; you may have been taught correctly, but often that is not the case. The longer perceived truth remains at the core of a person's belief system, the more it becomes connected to the self-identity of a person and the more difficult it is to change. Ultimately, it requires revelation of the Spirit to teach new and different things.

Preunderstanding may be so powerfully influenced by previous experiences that you tend to assume that is the only correct way to understand something in life, or the only way a verse can be interpreted. We immediately default to an interpretation that does little injury to our personal cultural norm. Our central beliefs and core values, which may require redefining an entire worldview, are harder to abandon than peripheral values.

This has all taken place before you even read and study a given biblical text. Though complete objectivity is impossible (we can't stop being who we are), the biggest caution is that unrestrained, wild, and free presuppositions will automatically limit your interpretive accuracy. How can we really find God's meaning if we keep injecting our own meaning?[2]

To separate religious words and thoughts from their original context makes them susceptible to manipulation and gross distortion. Commonly, dominant cultures tend to do just that looking for ways to make eternal truth subject to cultural truth, rather than make the temporal filter through the eternal.

---

[2] Eisegesis is the hermeneutical term for inserting something into the text that is not authentically there—that is, your own ideas.

There is on the reader-interpreter's part the moral responsibility to remain true to the essence of what God's truth conveys. We, as the honest reader-interpreter, must be willing to recognize there are limitations as to how far current application can be made and still remain biblical. Otherwise, the application exceeds the bounds of divine revelation and becomes cultural, humanistic, and philosophical in nature.

One of Augustine's most poignant observations states, *"If you believe what you like in the Gospel, and reject what you do not like, it is not the Gospel you believe, but yourself."*

Social Theologies and Scripture

A socio-cultural redefining of Christianity is now growing. In that redefining process, biblical Christianity is becoming less important, the church's historical practices are given less and less value, and the Bible is used little to provide meaningful direction and understanding for life's thorny issues. While normative biblical practices and values have come under relentless attack in this sweeping tidal wave of anti-traditional-biblical Christianity, socially interpreted theologies are on the rise.[3]

---

[3]Though not limited to these, these four are most prevalent: liberation theology (largely focused on class and economic inequalities); feminist theology (largely focused on systemic sexist's inequalities); political theology (largely interpreting Scripture by politics and empowerment to the disenfranchised; militarism is often found in this view); and revisionist gay theology (focused on deconstruction of the binary categories of sexual identity; in many writings it is called queer theology since much is taken from the queer theory philosophy). There is some overlap and commonality among all social theology.

Generally, the common thread among all social theologies is to conceptually dismiss basic biblical theology (God, Christ, redemption, etc.) for a theology based on making things just and right for all peoples (sin being defined as injustice). Their goals are to be accomplished through government and social reconstruction. Without question justice and equality are very important to God since justice and personal value are significant themes in both the OT and the NT. The problem is the approach social theologies suggest: challenging the concepts of God, Christ, salvation, the church, etc., as *inadequate or even false.*

In hope of not being too simplistic or minimizing life issues that are genuine and important, I believe social theologies make the strategic mistake of replacing and supplanting kingdom expectations of distinctive Christian behavior with philosophical subtleties as an adequate replacement. Social inequalities are real. Gender inequalities are real. Racial inequalities are real. Any meaningful solution to cultural problems will only be reached as sound biblical meaning and interpretation mold Christian life, not social theologies circumventing Scripture by the use of humanistic sensitivies.

Homosexual Reinterpretation of Scripture
No social group has been more aggressive in attempting to redefine Christianity and reinterpret Scripture than the gay community. In the past twenty-five years the LGBT

community has not only gained significant political and cultural strength but has made significant inroads in religion and biblical translations. Much of their growing acceptance has not been the result of sound biblical exegesis, but by political pressure, intimidation, and even assistance from a weakened American church threatened by being thought less loving and caring by these aggressive social theologies.

One of the LGBT community's most powerful and intimidating strategies is the vast overuse and distortion of the word *homophobic*.[4] With broad, sweeping generalities, anyone who holds a viewpoint about sexuality differing from theirs is labeled a homophobe or a bigot. While the LGBT community generalizes Christians as being homophobic, it steadfastly remains disingenuous about its own *theophobic*[5] stance. And therein lies the heart of the matter; their contempt for God and Scripture places the a spotlight on understanding the cultural distinctions between their homosexual culture and the Christian's kingdom culture.

The homosexual community's true agenda is not sexual freedom, nor cultural acceptance of alleged orientation; it

---

[4] The definition continues to broaden in society. It is now defined as any degree of dislike, prejudice, aversion to, fear of, or discrimination against (real or perceived) homosexuals and homosexuality.
[5] Theophobia is defined as fear of, hatred for, distaste for, or contempt for God and religion.

is independence from God. In November 2012, the Queen James Bible was introduced.[6] No editors are named, no supporting organization is named, but the mission of this edition is clear, "The Queen James Bible resolves any homophobic interpretation of the Bible, but the Bible is still filled with inequalities...that we did not address. You can't choose your sexuality, but you can choose Jesus. Now you can choose a Bible too." (From their website: queenjames bible.com.) The shaky, if not disingenuous, scholarship found in the rewriting of Scripture in the Queen James Bible is unmistakable.

In the QJB historical context is created where none exists; complete phrases are added that can be found in no other accepted manuscripts; and specific references to homosexual activities are deleted.[7] One of the defenses offered by supporters of the QJB is that the word *homosexuality* is not found in Scripture or is wrongly translated. But that position is part of the disingenuous scholarship and theology I mentioned in the previous paragraph. Let me explain further.

When the apostles directed first-century Christians to the Word of God, to what language and translation did they

---

[6] *The Queen James Bible, Study New Testament for Lesbians, Gay, Bi, and Transgender: The Inclusive Bible*, and *The First Egalitarian Bible* are just a sample of the growing number of Bibles and Bible study guides now available.

[7] They have targeted these specific verses for rewording to support their agenda (Gen. 19:5, Lev. 18:22, 20:13, Rom. 1:26–31, 1 Cor. 6:9–10, 1 Tim.1:10).

refer them? Since Hebrew ceased to be a commonly spoken language in 587 BCE, when Babylonian armies destroyed Jerusalem, the Torah and other holy texts began being translated into Greek. The Greek translation of the Hebrew Old Testament is called the Septuagint and was completed in 137 BCE. Paul's Scripture was the Septuagint. When Paul wrote of homosexuality as a sin and unacceptable behavior before God,[8] he used the same moral standard with the same word (*arsenokoites*[9]) that was used in Leviticus 20:13 in the Septuagint translation. The ritual laws of the OT were not carried over into the NT. However, God's moral laws were. They have never changed. God's moral law declared by Moses in Leviticus was repeated to the church by Paul without change in God's intent...and God's moral standard stands today.

Not every translation of Scripture uses the same English word for each Greek word; some translations interpret word for word (as much as is possible); others translate thought for thought. The commonly used word *trinity* is not found in Scripture, nor the word *rapture*, but the *doctrine* of both words is found in Scripture. As single words, *trinity* and *rapture* simply encapsulate the whole of the biblical teaching on their respective subjects. There just is no biblical teaching

---

[8] 1 Corinthians 6:9–10 and 1 Timothy 1:8–11.
[9] This is a compound word: *arseno*, meaning man or men and *koites*, meaning bed or sexual promiscuity.

in support of homosexual activities; in fact, OT and NT texts consistently warn against such behavior and label it sinful.

No portion of Scripture gives a more comprehensive overview of this spiritual battle between cultures than Romans 1. Paul identifies *purposeful* actions that indicate a desire to have an independent life apart from God, whether individually or as a collective community of like-minded individuals. In verses 18 through 20, he states that all men intrinsically and naturally know that God exists. The heavens and the earth are a cosmological portrait with God's signature at the bottom; but the wicked "suppress the truth" that creation testifies of God as the Creator. Thus the desire for independence from God begins....and quickly escalates into unrestrained sinful acts.

Cause and Effect in Romans 1, #1
- v. 18: they *suppressed* the truth—a conscious, willful act.
- v. 21: they *refused* to glorify God as God—a conscious, willful act.
- v. 22: they *exchanged* the living God for manmade images—a conscious, willful act.
- v. 24: "Therefore God gave them over in the sinful desires of their hearts to sexual impurity for the degrading of their bodies with one another."

Cause and Effect #2
- v. 25: they *rejected* God's truth to embrace a lie—a conscious, willful act.
- v. 26: "Because of this, God gave them over to shameful lusts. Even their women exchanged natural relations for unnatural ones. In the same way the men also abandoned natural relations with women and were inflamed with lust for one another."

Cause and Effect #3
- v. 28: they *rejected* knowledge of God as being worthwhile to retain—a conscious, willful act.
- v. 28: "He gave them over to a depraved mind, to do what ought not to be done."

God's judgment takes on a unique form for sexual impurity. It is not thunder and lightning, floods or tornadoes; He just releases them *from* His protection *to* what was already presently working, "the sinful desires of their heart." When God's Spirit and influence are rejected, men always turn to what is sensual. Sin becomes its own penalty; it is a downward spiral with the direst of consequences: the absence of God's presence.

When the LGBT community purposes to reject God's moral code, or even more blatantly God Himself, they do not leave sexual "appetite" in a vacuum. In lieu of moral guidelines based on divine principles they substitute moral values that are based upon sensuality or what feels "right." The problem is that what feels right is based upon hormones in the brain, and hormones are values-neutral. Hormones are amoral.

So, who sets moral values for amoral hormones that make things feel good? Someone must. God, the Creator of man? Anti-God communities? Who will set the moral values for sexual "appetite"? In the kingdom of God, He sets the moral values of what is or is not acceptable behavior, and that behavior is always in accord with His purposes expressed in the creating of man and woman before sin entered the equation. In any culture other than His, the moral values related to sexual activity have always been malleable to individual desires and the prevailing culture.

In his epistles, Paul creates four lists of human behavior that are vices directly connected to this topic of sexual expression:

- 1 Corinthians 5:11, "Anyone who calls himself a brother but is sexually immoral, etc."
- 1 Corinthians 6:9, "The wicked will not inherit the kingdom of God. Do not be deceived; neither the sexually immoral, etc."
- Galatians 5:19, "The acts of the sinful nature are obvious: sexual immorality, etc."
- Colossians 3:5, "Put to death whatever belongs to your earthly nature: sexual immorality, etc."

His pattern in each list identifies sexual immorality above all other vices. Paul's inclusive term *sexual immorality* does not make homosexual behavior or practice any worse than adultery, pornography, etc. The complexity of sin itself cannot be resolved with cookie cutter answers. But it is clear in human history that all sexual sins are devastating to people's lives and the fallout to others affected must also be considered in the toll sexual sin takes. Because sexual activity is so intimate and personal, the injury to others is also at a deep personal level. And because sexual sin posits those guilty persons against the original intent of God's creation for sex, the complexity of the issue is magnified. It is not just people-to-people...now God is involved.

Creative Design and Intent

Paul does not allow for shifting cultural standards on sexual activity to minimize God's creative intent. Homosexual behavior is defined by God as sin, *but the same acts are not necessarily considered sinful by the present culture* since this culture so readily endorses such behavior as normal and acceptable—as long as it is done in a loving relationship. Why is it that "loving" man-man or woman-woman relationships are not sufficient? Creative intent holds the key.

In all of human relationships, no other human intimacy better exhibits God's *original intent* than the sexual intimacy between a man and a woman. Created in His image and likeness, male and female in a sexual relationship are an *illustration of the intimacies possible between the human spirit and the divine Spirit*, God Himself. That picture of intimacy was God's primary purpose for the covenant relationship between a man and a woman. Paul makes this quite clear as he furthers the illustration using Christ and the church, the Groom and His bride: "This is a great mystery, but I speak concerning Christ and the church."[10] Giving Himself for her. Total trust. Total surrender. No other human relationship comes close. Loving sexual expressions between a husband and his wife are as much spiritual as they are physical. And this *designed relationship* produces fruit (children) for God's glory and fulfills His desire for a human family.

The LGBT community may even use some of these same words and descriptions for their own sexual relationships, but social restructuring is a far cry from divine design and assuredly misinterprets God's holiness. Because the human sexual relationship reflects the spiritual intimacies the human soul can have with God, Satan has targeted human sexuality for distortion, misunderstanding, abuse, and perversion like he has targeted no other human expression. Satan's only pleasure is to destroy what God has made. For the church to allow itself to be seduced or coerced into assimilation with the present culture of sexual

---

[10] Ephesians 5:22–33

immorality as being normal is a betrayal of divine love on a whole new level.

Egregious sexual immorality does not have the last word. Judgment does not have the last word. Compassion, mercy, and grace do:

> Or do you not know that the unrighteous will not inherit the kingdom of God? Do not be deceived: neither the sexually immoral, nor idolaters, nor adulterers, nor men who practice homosexuality, nor thieves, nor the greedy, nor drunkards, nor revilers, nor swindlers will inherit the kingdom of God. And such were some of you. *But you were washed, you were sanctified, you were justified in the name of the Lord Jesus Christ and by the Spirit of our God.*[11]

Homosexuality is anything but simple. It is a complex and multifaceted personal and social matter with increasing impact on today's global culture. There are two extreme postures that are problematic but between which hope can be found. On one side there are far too many in the church who find it difficult to believe that active homosexuals are capable of any sense of spirituality and Christ awareness. On the other side, most homosexuals have difficulty believ-

---

[11] 1 Corinthians 6:9–11 ESV

ing the church can be against homosexuality while at the same time being kind and loving toward homosexuals.

Whatever the LGBT community does, the church has only one viable course of action: to express with love and kindness the heart of God. The only weight of responsibility between the two groups *rests on the church*. If we in the church see homosexuals as sinners, *why would be surprised if they act like sinners*? But if we in the church are confrontational and loveless, *why should homosexuals believe we are Christian*?

Gender-Specific Translations

Gender-specific translations of Scripture may scratch the present-day itch, but that endeavor completely misses the comprehensive depth of value God places on both genders. The apostle Paul addresses the issue head-on. To everyone who becomes a child of God through faith in Jesus Christ[12] they can expect radical social upheaval. The upheaval will be *within* the Christ-born person's own mind and heart as their old culture is forced to give way to God's new culture. The cultural markers of their old life must be cast aside. Their old values and norms will have no place in their new kingdom culture. *"There is neither Jew nor Greek, slave nor free, male nor female, for you are all one in Christ."*[13]

---

[12] Galatians 3:26
[13] Galatians 3:28 (NIV). Paul expresses the same principle to the church in Colossae (3:11).

To Jews, masters, and males, entrance into the kingdom of God may not have seemed like "good news"; in Christ, gentiles, slaves, and women were given equal standing. *That is radical.* Every generation has found the person of Christ and the kingdom message of Christ to be culturally subversive.

The most obvious cultural distinctions the apostle addressed were:

- Jews/non-Jews   or   ethnicity-race
- Slave/free   or   social status
- Male/female   or   gender

Each of these three realities gave advantage to some while leaving its counterpart on the outside looking in. To the outsider, the culturally disenfranchised, the barriers were simply impassable. What levels the playing field is Jesus Christ. In Christ no one race or ethnic group is advantaged over any other; no particular social status is advantaged over any other; and no gender prevails over the other. All things have become new in Christ…*and equal.*

Paul does not ask believers to ignore the distinctions their eyes see, but he does require them *now* to see the other party as an equal in Christ. His requirement is for Christians to live differently and seek reconciliation with others (formerly seen as beneath them) because they now have a new life in Christ. Paul broadens his position to the church in Corinth, "So from now on we regard no one from a worldly point of view."[14]

Male and Female Tensions

The oldest distinction is the last on his list: male–female. It long predated ethnicity, race, and social status, "So God created man in his own image...male and female he created them."[15] Consequently, it is that long-term gender conflict I will speak to. The other distinctions are covered in broad fashion above in the footnote concerning social theologies.

To be overly sensitized to the word *man* in Scripture exposes a cultural bias that discounts the equal value God places on male-female *as he created them*. "He created them male and female and *blessed them*. And when they were created, he *called them 'man.'*"[16] When God uses the term *man*, He is referencing "male-female" as the combined expression of His creative act. God's created intrinsic value for male-female is the same; God's created intrinsic blessing for male-female is the same; God's eternal value on each gender is the same.

God's design of complementary oneness was turned topsy-turvy by the serpent's deception in Eden. It only begins to

---

[14] 2 Corinthians 5:16 (NIV)
[15] Genesis 1:17 (NIV)
[16] Genesis 5:2

be restored in Christ. Any personal or cultural belief system outside Christ's mutual equality will continue to feed the battle of the sexes.

Gender inequalities outside the body of Christ are primarily one-dimensional; they pertain to this present natural life. NT theology, particularly Paul's, emphasizes the repetitive call for believers to bring the future into the present. What God has ordained for the eternal *spiritual* realm is now to invade the present *natural* realm as God's model for value, significance, and equality. Cultural distinctions are to be superseded by oneness and unity in a new kingdom culture; eternal values are to override temporary cultural values.

Christians living out the future in the present offer the only hopeful answer to such a tension-filled issue. Obviously, there is a sharp contradiction between God's designed complementary wholeness in gender equality and man-made divisive barriers of gender inequality. The apostolic writings of Paul, Peter, and John were to restore what God intended and man's sin demolished. This culturally generated hotspot is not unlike my initial question: How can you live in two worlds at the same time? Gender fits the same format: How do you live in a world as male or female and in another world (at the very same moment) where there is neither male nor female?

As new creations in Christ, believers are to embrace the gender they now possess (male or female) in a manner of life that is spiritual *and* natural. Principles of the Word and the Spirit are to guide and lead life in the present natural state, lived to God's glory as His representatives of kingdom culture. The Spirit's new life culture replaces old societal structures that foster "rights" and "position." Through his guiding we are to live in the here and now as if we are living in the yet-to-come.

One's value and significance is no longer gender value, which on one hand can easily be prideful or dominating, while on the other hand can be divisive, or repressive. In the Lord, male-female are simultaneously one in value and significance while being uniquely different in creative design. *Roles are different; value is not.* Dominant cultures have historically been structured in such a way that class tension, economic tension, or gender tension resulted. The message of the gospel restores insight into God's original creative intent for equality: male and female created in His image and likeness. Based upon His redemptive plan in Christ Jesus, both male and female are to embrace their sexuality as an expression of His nature, lived in His honor.

Equal and complementary values found in Christ are just no longer based on class, birth, or gender. To the degree Christians actually practice the in-Christ model of mutual respect and appreciation and the accepting of equal value and significance, self-seeking rule, battling for position, and dominance will be minimized. Only the naïve would suggest it would completely disappear. But if each Christian male lives his "maleness" to God's glory and majesty and each female lives her "femaleness" to God's glory and majesty, they will best reflect God's purpose.

Distinctions in the natural realm will always remain, but those distinctions should have *less* exploitation and totalitarianism when the in-Christ model prevails. Paul's words need to be repeated frequently: "In Christ there is neither male nor female" and "From now on we regard no one from a worldly point of view."

"Intellectual darkness comes through ignorance; spiritual darkness comes because of something I do not intend to obey."

Oswald Chambers
My Utmost for His Highest

· 7 ·

Sex, Lusts, and Fantasies
Part 1

This present generation commonly has been called the addicted generation. Topping the list are being addicted to technology, addicted to drugs, and addicted to sex. In general public use, using the term *addiction* is somewhat misleading since it is normally used in a nonclinical sense. But it comes close enough as people use the term to describe a culture that is preoccupied and absorbed with *something*.

As to technology, preoccupation with the Internet, digital devices, video games, and cell phones is a fascination that would not have been available to previous generations, though this generation seems quite determined to make up for lost time.

As to drugs, archeologists have found evidence that drug abuse and addiction predate alphabets and written languages. But damage done by drug abuses in previous generations does not seem to be a lesson learned by *any* generation, including this one. Recreational drugs and prescription drugs are grossly abused, and both hold the risk of addiction.

As to sex addiction, it is actually not always easy to track as an *addiction* because of the promiscuity and indiscriminate casual sex that are so common to this generation. Making unbounded sex normal can mask a genuine problem. Unfortunately, the church has also been caught in the cultural vise of assimilation at the cost of holy distinction. The lordship of Christ *should be seen* in every believer's sexual experience, but too frequently it is not. The apostle Paul made it clear that sexual activity *cannot be separated* from divine intent and divine awareness.

> Flee from sexual immorality. All other sins a person commits are outside the body, but whoever sins sexually, sins against their own body. Do you not know that your bodies are temples of the Holy Spirit, who is in you, whom you have received from God? You are not your own; you were bought at a price. Therefore honor God with your bodies.[1]

Expressing our human sexuality without restraints or boundaries (whether single or married) is to miss the context of sexual expression God initiated in Eden with Adam and Eve. Sexual activity is not merely an emotional and physical expression that can be exercised apart from the whole of my being, or apart from God either.

---

[1] 1 Corinthians 6:18–20

The World's Most Famous Sexual Escapade

There are some very obvious lessons for twenty-first Christians to learn from the horrific story of David and Bathsheba. The story is egregiously devastating on many levels that are not immediately obvious but become clearer with a little biblical investigation.

If this story is so ugly, why is it in the Bible? Is David's story recorded in 2 Samuel to let us know that a good man can go bad? We don't need this story to prove that point; good, upright people fail every day. Second Samuel 11:1 begins this story by letting us know it is the spring of the year, the time when kings would normally go to battle. But David didn't go that year. He stayed home. A number of Bible and history scholars have done a lot of sermonizing and spiritualizing about the kings-go-to-war-in-the-Spring scenario, but that misses the point entirely. Hindsight certainly proves staying home that year was undoubtedly a bad decision on David's part—or did the decision to stay home *really* have much to do with this at all? What is *the real point* in this ugly story?

Look at this closely. David is pushing sixty years old...at the very youngest he is in his mid-fifties. David is not a novice with little life experience and who has unwittingly been seduced by some wily, crafty woman. He has evolved from an unknown shepherd, to a national hero, to an internationally known warrior...and is now king himself. This story begins with a very disturbing revelation: *Bathsheba was*

*young enough to be his granddaughter...and she was not
a stranger!*

Who Was Bathsheba to David?

David demanded the sexual favors of a young woman he
knew very, very well. It appears he may not have immediately recognized her across the rooftops, but he was quickly
made aware of who she was by one of his servants.[2] Even
knowing *exactly* who she was did not deter David from his
uncontrolled passions; the king still demanded her presence. That one little piece of the story reveals the depths of
how far David had fallen. If there was the slightest hesitation
about the identity of the woman he was demanding, when
she walked into his room, all doubt was removed. He knew
Bathsheba as:

- the *granddaughter* of his *personal* advisor;
- the *daughter* of one of his *personal* bodyguards; and
- the *wife* of still another of his *personal* bodyguards.

Follow the biblical trail of these relationships:
- It begins with his personal counselor, Ahithophel:
  "Ahithophel, the Gilonite, David's counselor"
  (2 Sam 15:12).

---

[2] 2 Sam. 11:3

- Then the trail leads us to Ahithophel's son Eliam, one
  of David's thirty personal bodyguards. *"...the son of
  Ahithophel the Gilonite."* (2 Sam 23:34).
- Then what do we discover? She is Eliam's daughter and
  Ahithophel's granddaughter! *"Is this not Bathsheba, the
  daughter of Eliam"* (2 Sam. 11:3).
- Then we discover she also was the wife of another of
  David's personal bodyguards, Uriah. *"Is this not
  Bathsheba, the daughter of Eliam, the wife of Uriah the
  Hittite?"* (2 Sam. 11:3).
- Uriah completed the list of the elite palace guard who
  protected the king with their very lives. *"Uriah the Hittite:
  thirty and seven in all"* (2 Sam. 23:39).
- Ahithophel was the father of Eliam, who was the father of
  Bathsheba, who was the wife of Uriah.
- Ahithophel served David as personal counselor; Eliam
  and Uriah served David as personal bodyguards.

Murder and the Light of God

The interpretation of Uriah's name is more than ironic; it
is a bit chilling in view of this story: his name means
"Yahwah is my light." Just think about that for a moment!
With an act of almost unthinkable betrayal, David had
the light of God snuffed out; the symbolism here is deep
and revealing. What's happening inside this man? This is
betrayal at an unspeakable level! Only an insensitive and
self-centered man could possibly betray those whose very
lives were committed to keeping him safe from *any* and *all*

dangers. Every day David's elite bodyguard unit put their lives on the line for him, willing to sacrifice theirs for his.

Uriah had done nothing but serve his king with loyal devotion. It seems with the introduction of each new character in this story the darkness in David's heart becomes more startling. Uriah's death is the capstone. David's actions are a cold-blooded, premeditated murder designed to cover up the sleazy, perverted behavior of a national leader. This once-trusted leader is now driven by the compelling motive that the woman of his one-night stand is pregnant. This leader also has ready means to facilitate the hiding of his scandalous behavior, and that behavior becomes a compelling part of this story.

David's military mind quickly conceived a foolproof cover-up to what he had done; he insisted General Joab implement his strategy on the field of battle. Joab was to put Uriah in the front of the assault and then abandon him; the consequences were clearly predictable. Kill her husband...end of problem. Get rid of Uriah, "the light of God."

An Abuse of Power

As king, David held life and death in his will and word. Speak the word and a person's life would continue...or end...at his sole discretion. How much resistance could a woman offer in the face of such unlimited and unquestioned power? In her culture absolutely no complaint from her about, or toward, the king would ever be tolerated! If she simply smiled wrong he could end her life; to deny his demands was certain death. The king had *demanded* her presence!

David's abuse of his position put an entire family at risk. If she resisted, what would happen to her grandfather? Would his position be in jeopardy? What might happen to her father? Would he be demoted? And what about her husband? Bathsheba would never have imagined that the man who wrote songs to God would have him murdered. Remember, her family members were not strangers to the king. Their lives, careers, income, and future were uniquely interwoven into this demand of David.

When power is abused as egregiously as this, be assured someone other than the abuser is going to pay the price. Bathsheba must have surely hoped that a quiet acquiescence to David's demands would help minimize any potentially devastating effects for her and her family. But whether it would or would not, she simply had no choice but to respond to the king's demands.

A Sex Drive Out of Control
Or is the story about David and Bathsheba actually the story of a man simply unable to control his sexual lust and who then finds that lust has driven him to adultery? Is this the story of a man with a lifelong sexual proclivity? There may be some biblical evidence to support that thought, as you

will see. Whatever other unresolved issues were working deep within David, the manifestation of those unknowns was clearly seen in his sexual propensities. Personally, I would be hard pressed to believe that David was not familiar with the three prohibitions for Israel's kings as listed in Deuteronomy 17:16–18. So significant is the threefold warning to Israel's future kings that Moses further mandated in verse 18 that when the king sits on the throne of the kingdom, "He shall write for himself in a book a copy of this law... it shall be with him, and he shall read it all the days of this life." Look at these imperatives:

1. The kings of Israel were not to "multiply, acquire, or increase" *horses*. Horses were the symbols of power, military might. But the king of Israel was not to put his trust in horses for national defense. Protection of the nation was to be trusting faith *in I AM*—the name above every name. David understood this. Just read his own words in Psalm 20:7, "Some trust in chariots, and some in horses: but we will remember the name of the Lord our God."

2. The kings of Israel were not to "multiply, acquire, or increase" *wives*. That verse in Deuteronomy not only gives a very plain prohibition but also makes equally clear the reason why multiple women were not to be drawn into the king's life: "lest his heart turn away" (ESV) "his heart will be led astray" (NIV). The spiritual danger far exceeded the benefits of political alliances through marriage; it

warns directly of the king's heart being turned away from God by other intimacies. Biblical texts that refer to "foreign wives" are those women not under Israel's covenant. Foreign wives bring foreign theologies.

3. The kings of Israel were not to "multiply, acquire, or increase" *gold and silver.* A great temptation to vanity and self-gratification seems to accompany massive wealth. Buy whatever you want, whenever you want. It becomes easy to think you can buy your way into any place, or out of any situation. But Jehovah-Jireh was to be the only source of trust and provision for the kings. Their dependency was an opportunity for Him to show Himself strong and faithful to the people of Israel. David understood this as well. All through his songs David sings *warnings about personal vanity and the need to remain encouraged in God alone.*

But it is the second prohibition given to Israel's kings that seems to be David's snare—the one that seems to put the spotlight on his sexual compulsion. Minimally it seems to highlight his uncontrolled need for women. If David had practiced *just a few* of the many moral truths he wrote to the Lord, this nightmare would never have happened.

> Keep your servant also from willful sins; may they not rule over me. Then I will be blameless, innocent of great

transgression. May the words of my mouth and the meditations of my heart be pleasing in your sight, O Lord.[3]

Stand in awe, and sin not: commune with your own heart upon your bed, and be still.[4]

How Many?

But for David, application of that truth seems to be selective. The mandate from Moses seems lost on David; he had eight wives we know by name! Here are the first seven:

1. Michael (1 Sam.18:27), who was barren
2. Abigail (1 Sam. 25:42), mother of Daniel
3. Ahinoam (1 Sam. 25:43), mother of Amnon
4. Maachah (2 Sam. 3:3), mother of Absalom
5. Haggith (2 Sam. 3:4), mother of Adonijah
6. Abital (2 Sam. 3:4), mother of Shephatiah
7. Eglah (2 Sam. 3:5), mother of Ithream

And what about the wives whose names we *do not know*! How many of them were there? In addition to the unknown wives, how many concubines did David have?

And David took more concubines and wives out of Jerusalem."[5]

---

[3] Ps. 19:13,14
[4] Ps. 4:4
[5] 2 Samuel 5:13

His collection of wives and concubines, in violation of Moses's imperative to kings, took place *before* we get to this sad and pathetic part of David's life. *Now*, after all these wives and concubines have shared his bed, we come to the eighth wife, whose name is revealed in Scripture. This woman would only become available for David to marry because David had ruthlessly snuffed out the *"light of God."*

Who was wife number eight? Bathsheba, the wife of Uriah.

- mother of the baby who died from the adulterous affair
- mother of Solomon
- mother of Shammua
- mother of Shabob
- mother of Nathan[6]

What God Saw

We have now reviewed all the characters central to this story, except one. We have seen how David's sin impacted the life and future of all characters central to this story, except one: God, David's God. It is God's perspective that shows what is really going on behind the scenes in David's sexual escapade. It is God's perspective that shows our own sins have another side, things not so obvious to us. God was not ignorant of the obvious sins David committed:

---

[6] All of David's children are listed in 1 Chronicles 3. Verse 5 lists the four sons born to him by Bathsheba

- uncontrolled lust and passion
- abuse of position and power
- betrayal of trust and friendship
- calloused indifference
- adultery
- murder

But He sent the prophet Nathan to make clear the far-reaching scope of what was really going on: *"By this deed thou hast given great occasion to the enemies of the Lord to blaspheme."* That phrase in Hebrew carries the meaning, *"By this deed you have given great cause for dishonor to bloom like a flower among my enemies."*

Every one of us has stories we could tell about the devastation and impact of sexual sin we have witnessed in lives other than the active partners. We of the clergy try to heal and mend the spouses and children who are left broken in the wake of such betrayal. We often fail. These are innocent lives that are forever changed; relationships once strong are now broken and may never be healed. All too often the lost trust can never be regained. Tears. Grief. Pain. Anger. Despair. Bitterness.

Do you think Ahithophel, David's long-time personal counselor, forgot the anguish of his son, Eliam? Do you think he forgot the trauma and turmoil that was forced upon his granddaughter, Bathsheba? Do you think he was indifferent to the gut-wrenching pain when he was informed that his granddaughter was pregnant by the king? Do you think he forgot his own crushing sense of betrayed loyalty and friendship as he watched David run roughshod over his entire family? How could he possibly forget the murder of his grandson-in-law, Uriah? He didn't.

Just a few short years later when Absalom was determined to remove his father as king and take the throne for himself, as Absalom planned his coup, he invited Ahithophel to abandon David's side and join him. Ahithophel jumped at the opportunity to exact revenge on the man who had so devastated his family.[8]

Ahithophel definitely was a man you wanted on your team; wise, perceptive, and godly. In fact the Scripture says that when Ahithophel spoke it was like God speaking! "For every word Ahithophel spoke seemed as wise as though it had come directly from the mouth of God."[9]   But the deep wounding from David had never healed, so he joined the conspiracy to remove David from the throne—and hopefully excise him from his life and his family's agony.

David learned a sense of God's grace he had not known be-fore, but the price was high. It was a price without end: "the

---

[8] 2 Samuel 15:12, 31
[9] 2 Samuel 16:23 (NLT)

sword never left David's house."[10] Murder, rape, betrayal, and anarchy among his own children marked the family the remainder of David's life. God forgave David, but forgiveness did not erase life's consequences.

God sees what we do to other people. He sees what our sin does to the immediate family, to faithful and trusting friends, the church, even the community. But our sin has still greater consequences than what is done to people...the thing we don't see as clearly, the thing not so obvious is, *"By this deed you have caused dishonor to bloom like a flower among my enemies."*

---

[10] 2 Samuel 12:10

"For any happiness, even in this world, quite a lot of restraint is going to be necessary... every sane and civilized man must have some set of principles by which he chooses to reject some of his desires and to permit others. The real conflict is not between Christianity and 'nature,' but between Christian principle and other principles in the control of 'nature.'"

C. S. Lewis
Mere Christianity

· 8 ·

Sex, Lusts, and Fantasies
Part 2

Where do you find the enemies of God? You don't have to search hard or long to locate them; they are all around us and can be found in both the natural realm and spiritual realm. When we sin, we give occasion for the natural enemies of God to mock, jeer, and *dishonor His name*. We also give His spiritual enemies the same prime opportunity. Our world is eager to magnify everything it can that might make the church look bad or the name of Jesus inept—anything to dishonor His name! It's as if they are on high alert to find any and every chance to do this. In other words, they are watching *us*!

Exodus 32 provides a great illustration of this. As Moses and Joshua returned from meeting with God, "Moses saw that the people were running wild and that Aaron had let them get out of control and so become a laughingstock to their enemies."[1] Israel's enemies were God's enemies, and when mocking these so-called "different" people they were also mocking their "different" God. They were watching the

---

[1] Exodus 32:25 NIV

actions of God's people and forming opinions of Israel's God based on their *"running wild"* behavior!

Just a few years ago an elderly man was charged with sexual child abuse here in the Dallas area. The bold, glaring headline of this story in the local newspaper didn't say, "old man charged," it didn't say "elderly man charged," and it didn't say "senior citizen charged." The headline read, "Pastor's Father Charged with Sexually Abusing Child"— just a little spin to make it look worse and bring *dishonor* to the name of the Lord.

Was the headline deliberately written to dishonor? I don't know. It may not have even been a conscious consideration by the editor. But for the enemies of God who have their radar attuned to this sort of thing, it certainly gave *"great occasion for dishonor to blossom like a flower."* And that's just *one* local story. Unfortunately, there continue to be others every so often in our local media. But not just here— they seem to appear in every community across the nation. Drugs. Sex. Fraud. Embezzlement. More flowers blooming.

That news story was about a man hardly known outside his immediate circle of family and friends. But how in the world do you begin to measure the dishonor that is done to the name of our God when the sin of a highly visible, nationally known preacher is exposed? It feeds and energizes the enemies of God for weeks and months, sometimes for years. From television sitcoms, radio talk shows, magazines, newspapers, water cooler talk, to late night stand-up comics, ridicule and sarcasm *(dishonor)* seem to be never ending.

It has been almost thirty years since the Jim Baker and Jimmy Swaggart sexual failures fed the evening news and empowered the enemies of God. To this day those two men are still referred to by the enemies of God in ways that continue to dishonor Him. God's enemies don't talk about the repentance of these men, God's forgiveness, or their restoration. We in the church family *might*. We ought to be humbled by such acts of divine mercy and divine love toward these men. We ought to be awed in seeing the heart of God show such faithful love and restoration. We ought to learn that character must be more important than success. But God's enemies have no compassion for failure when saints do the failing.

To the enemies of God, it was far more than the obvious moral failure of these church leaders; it was a *"great occasion for dishonor to blossom like a flower."* Unfortunately, God's enemies continue to water it and keep it alive. That flower still blooms. The ripples of sexual sin by Ted Haggard, the pastor of a mega-church in Colorado, an internationally known speaker and writer, and the then president of the National Association of Evangelicals, are still popping up in the news years later. How long will that plant of dishonor bloom?

A Loss of Trust

A generation ago the top two professions held in highest esteem were clergy and doctors. In this generation's list of the top 100 professions and how they are respected and esteemed, doctors have slipped a few slots. The clergy? Clergy members have dropped like a rock. They now rank number 53 for being "trustworthy and held in esteem." *Number 53!* To say American clergy have an image problem is an understatement; to say the American church has an image problem is an understatement.

The growing negative perception of Christianity is not the *non-Christians'* fault; it is ours. When our actions and attitudes give false representation of a holy God, it is no wonder that God is mocked and Christianity is considered hypocritical. That is the collective view. But what about me…what about you? Moral failures, sexual uncleanness, and uncontrolled lust all are egregious in nature—but they are not the real issue! This is the real issue: *Have I given the enemies of God an opportunity to dishonor Him? Have you?* This goes far beyond sex, lust, and fantasies.

It would be very easy to shift blame to reporters, media outlets, stand-up comics, and anyone else who makes these tragic sins a vicious public matter. It would be easy to defensively suggest they tend to make it worse than it really is. But don't get too upset with God's enemies too quickly. They may seem to take great delight in reporting it and keeping it alive, but don't lose sight of this fact: *the media did not commit the sin!* We did. In John's seven letters to the churches of Asia Minor recorded in the book of Revelation, each letter was addressed to a specific church as a corporate body, while clearly recognizing that not everyone in that church was guilty of the charges brought by the Lord Jesus. By using the identifier "we" as the people of God, I am not suggesting that everyone in the clergy, or everyone sitting in the pew, is guilty of such sexual misconduct. But there is a bond and link between us as the one family of God (regardless of affiliation or denominational name) that is unique to the body of Christ, and when such sinful behavior is made public, the stigma affects all of us.

Who Needs to Know?

It is not uncommon for the first response of the people involved in sexual misconduct to deny it happened and keep it secret—*just like David did.* But that does no one any good! I am not suggesting that the local church take out a full-page ad in the newspaper to announce the moral failure of the pastor, a staff member, or an elder or even the sins of a person sitting on the last pew in the church. But I am saying that to hide it and bury it doesn't deal with repentance or provide opportunities for restoration and corporate healing. And it certainly in no way begins to deal with the dishonor that is brought to our God.

Exposure of sin with the intent of repentance and restoration does not dishonor God! If that were true, God would have become a participant in keeping David's sin under wraps. If secrecy and cover-up were legitimate strategies for God, several stories in Scripture absolutely *would have been omitted.* If all Scripture is given by inspiration of the Holy Spirit, as Paul wrote, the Holy Spirit *made sure* these accounts were included, *not excluded.*

It was only after the confrontation by Nathan that David was able to bring himself to a place of honesty and humility before the Lord. Secrecy would *never* have allowed that to take place. These things don't just happen in the church. Someone *always* must take the lead or be the instigator in this type of sin...and he or she always does it covertly. But once it is known, secrecy is *never* an option if it is to be handled God's way—a way that brings restoration and wholeness.

The church is not so much in denial as it is in control. I have observed church officials, in their secrecy mode, castigate and ostracize the person who revealed the sin, which creates a fearful culture of silence, while attempting at the same time to keep in the shadows the "doer" and avoid the spotlight of exposure on his or her God-dishonoring deeds. *Why?* I have seen denominational leaders cover up such sin and move a pastor on to another place so it wouldn't be made public. *Why?*

There are two primary reasons why church and denominational leaders go into damage control with such secrecy: first, fear of a lawsuit from which a church might never recover financially; and second, as much as possible to protect the church's image in the community from which a church might never recover. We live in a very litigious society, and unfortunately the threat of lawsuits from *within the church membership* has become an all-too-real concern. The impact of sexual scandal is so powerful that there are some churches that just cannot be stabilized again. Their once-sterling image is gone; their community effectiveness is gone; their spiritual health is gone; and their oneness of loving, trusting community is gone. Weakness has replaced strength.

Which Honors God: Truth or Cover-Up?
As real as those two present-day fears may be, I believe those two things hardly create a blip on God's radar. The Holy Spirit directed Paul to instruct the church that the sins of an elder were to be made known to the church so others could learn by it! As strange as it may sound, I believe the voice of the world has been used by God to challenge we believers to deal with sin issues more pointedly than we tend to do on our own if left un-prodded. They won't let us cover it up! Thank God.

It's this simple: the enemies of God who jump on these opportunities are not acting out of character in the eyes of God. They are simply being true to what they are. They make no claims about being "different," "born again," or "a new man in Christ." In fact the very idea of personally embracing any of these concepts is repugnant to many of them. It's God's own child that gives *them* opportunity to dishonor *Him*.

God made it very clear that *David*, and he alone, had given His enemies this "great occasion." Not one word does God have to say about Bathsheba. Nathan the prophet has no message for her. No rebuke...nothing. So don't even waste your time trying to conjure up some way for blame to be shared. God had the source pinpointed. When you and I sin, *the real issue identified in heaven* is not lust, uncontrolled sexual urges, erotic fantasies, an emotional affair, a physical affair—as bad as those are. It is much, much more. *We have dishonored God before His enemies.*

Charles Spurgeon said, "Let the minister who commits sexual sin, sit on the back pew until his repentance is as well known as his sin." In the nineteenth century, ministers who committed sexual sin were removed from the pulpit, not because they were such poor preachers but because they were such poor examples of being a Christian.

What if it's private and no one finds out about it? If I keep it only in my mind, who knows? If I engage in a little porn surfing on my computer, who knows? If I do a little looking and no touching, who knows? Who cares? God is very much aware of what I think and say within myself. I may never speak my thoughts aloud; I may even be afraid to speak them because God may hear. How deluded and shallow to discount God's all knowing!

For the LORD searches every heart and understands every desire and every thought.[2]

I the LORD search the heart and examine the mind, to reward each person according to their conduct, according to what their deeds deserve.[3]

Enemies in the Heavenlies

There is still another class of enemies that takes great delight in dishonoring God. The *spiritual enemies* of God: powers, principalities, demons, devils, unclean spirits, fallen angels, and any other biblical name (or synonym) you wish to use. The apostle Paul said we do not wrestle with flesh and blood; ergo, our real enemies are spiritual, not physical. What we may see and hear from God's earthly physical enemies (mocking, laughing, jeers, ridicule, swearing, joke telling, slander, gossip—all expressions of *dishonor*) are loud, boisterous manifestations of these *spiritual enemies* feeding, encouraging, and working their eternal dishonor *through* physical men.

---

[2] 1 Chronicles 28:9
[3] Jeremiah 17:10

These spiritual enemies are just using men to manifest what is taking place in the spirit world—*dishonor to God.* The *"great occasion"* brought about by my sin, your sin. *It's all about honor!* What you and I do either honors or dishonors His majesty. Period. Over and over in Scripture these words are found: "for your name's sake" or "for His name's sake." You may as well be saying, *"For Your honor's sake."*

Unguarded moments are not insignificant! Every believer has to take seriously the consequences of sinful action. Our focus needs to expand from how these actions affect us personally, our families, and begin to see the bigger picture. I have *never* met a believer who *consciously decided* to dishonor God by sexual misconduct:

- I think I will deliberately do something today that's erotic and off color that will dishonor the Lord.
- Let's see, I think I'll have an affair today, just to dishonor my Father.
- Maybe I'll just flirt a little with my secretary, just a little erotic titillation so His enemies can mock Him.
- I wonder how many women I can "accidentally" brush up against today so dishonor will blossom.
- What can I wear today that will "turn on" all the men…so my Father's enemies can laugh?

We just don't think that way! We simply do not see life that way! *But God's spiritual enemies do!* The hosts of "rulers of the darkness" take satanic glee when we ignorantly act without seeing the full consequences of our acts. It's not so much that we are always *totally* ignorant of what we are doing, but we are *terribly* ignorant of the magnitude of the consequences. These unseen enemies of God readily jump on every *"great occasion"* we provide them to dishonor Him.

Guidelines of Honor
Paul was very concerned about proper relationships in the church and directed Timothy to teach on this matter:

> Do not rebuke an older man harshly, but exhort him as if he were your father. Treat younger men as brothers, older women as mothers, and younger women as sisters, with absolute purity.[4]

I really like the way the NIV ends this passage: *"with absolute purity."* That would include purity of heart, purity of thought, purity of intent, purity of emotions, purity in looks, smiles, and gestures. That's the way we as believers are to interact with each other—so that honor is given to God.

Peter just nails it. There is a distinctive mandate in his epistles that Christians must embrace a higher moral code of living, which thereby empowers ethical obligations to live Christ-like. Those transformed in Christ give their greatest

---

[4] 1 Timothy 5:1–2

witness by their conduct, not their speaking. Through Peter's lens, a minister's greatest sermon is outside the pulpit, not in it. Simply put, those who "according to the fore-knowledge of God the Father, in the sanctification of the Spirit, for obedience to Jesus Christ"[5] are expected to live differently—sanctified and obedient.

The apostolic fathers watched the growing influence of Gnosticism grip the young church in the form of false teachers who claimed to have revelation of higher knowledge. The tension within the Gnostics themselves seemed to have no middle ground; they either purported ascetic restraint to one's flesh or released unfettered sexual freedoms. Peter goes to the heart of the matter as he addresses those in the church who are being ensnared by the attraction to unfettered sexual freedom.

If the body has no important role to play in living out one's salvation, why ever say no to sexual pleasure? He cautions them of the real danger of their sexual sin: "Many will follow their sensuality and because of them *the way of truth will be blasphemed.*"[6] The NIV says they will bring the way of the truth "into disrepute."

That is the real consequence of our sin!

---

[5] 1 Peter 1:2 NIV
[6] 2 Peter 2:2 ESV

God's message to David was a real spiritual-eye-opener. There is much more going on than our normal reading of his erotic escapades. God's enemies are watching, waiting to pounce on our foolish unrestrained behavior. A constant reminder to live for God's glory and honor would go a long way in keeping us all safe from sexual fantasies becoming egregious unretractable actions. Beyond sex, lust, and fantasies, it is much more important to keep the flowers of dishonor from blooming.

Ultimately, my living it is more about God than it is about me.

One last word: for some divinely inexplicable reason, the moral failures of some are exposed and the moral failures of others are not. For whatever grace God sovereignly expresses in allowing our sins to remain secret (between us and Him), those so blessed should live in private regret and public humility.

"The twin deceivers of the Christian life are success and failure. God has called us to neither. He has called us to faithfulness."

Oswald Chambers
My Utmost for His Highest

· **9** ·

Who Determines Success: Our Culture or Our God?

Recently I removed all the old Bible markers from the three Bibles I regularly use and replaced them with new ones; the new ones I had recently picked up at the Dallas County Forensics Laboratory. My new Bible markers are *toe tags* from the county morgue. Honest. For several days I had been reading through Paul's letters and was struck in a new way his words *"you are dead," "mortify," "crucified with Christ," "old man," "new man," "new creation," "buried,"* and of course the clincher, *"reckon the old man dead."*

When I called the morgue, I identified myself to the man who answered the phone and told him why I was calling… and he immediately began to laugh.

"Excuse me, but did I miss something here?"

"No, no. It's just that I get a lot of calls for these. Doctors. Policemen. But you're the first preacher that has ever called wanting toe tags."

When I met this fine doctor in his very quiet workplace, I quickly discovered a toe tag is not *just* a toe tag. There are multiple toe tags—different colors of toe tags. Toe tag number one was not a surprise. It was just what I expected: light tan in color and used for those people who had died in non-suspicious ways (in a hospital, under hospice care, etc.).

He then handed me toe tag number two. I didn't know there was a number two. This one was the same light tan color but with a bold red border and used for the "John Does" and "Jane Does" who find their way onto his table. The unknown persons with an unknown history needed to be distinctive from the known persons.

Ahhh, but toe tag number three. The doctor's explanation made it clear why I was there following my heart's strange leading, and he also helped me connect my impressions to Paul's writings. Number three was an unmistakable, easy-to-be-seen, bright fluorescent green. You can't miss it. They don't *want* you to miss it!

In big black letters it reads: **Blood Precautions— Infectious Hazard**

The doctor explained why this tag was made to stand out, *"This one we put on the person who is dead, but still dangerous. He's dead, but he can still kill you."* Infectious. Now dead. Still dangerous. This was not a tongue-in-cheek or humorous moment for me. Something from Paul's theology became crystal clear to me. I'm dead. You're dead. We're all dead. This is a world of walking talking dead people—not part of the current zombie craze from Hollywood, but as a picture of spiritual identification.

The Walking Dead

I am dead in Christ, or I am dead in trespasses and sin. Me. You. All of us. In the first death I give honor to God; in the second I dishonor Him. Every time I pick up my Bible and move a new toe tag, I am now visibly reminded that I am faced with choices:

- Choice 1: to be crucified with Christ, walk in the Spirit, be dangerous to the devil, and honor God.

- Choice 2: to be dead in sin, walk in the flesh, be dangerous to the people around me, and dishonor God.

If I walk in the death that leads to new life, I infect people with my encouragement, faith, confidence, hope, love, steadiness, truth, grace, and kindness. If I walk in the death that leads to deeper death, I infect people with my discouragement, unbelief, criticism, gossip, anger, harshness, impatience, and know-it-all attitude. I build them up or I tear them down. My choice. My infection. In fact, I am now convinced that disciples of Christ are not dangerous until they are dead. Only the dead are truly productive for the kingdom of God, and only the dead can truly live for His honor and

His glory. Jesus did not die to make us comfortable; He died to make us dangerous.

> Truly, truly, I say unto you, unless a grain of wheat fall into the ground and *dies*, it remains alone; *but if it dies, it bears much fruit.*[1] (emphasis mine)

It's more than being productive or even successful; it's about honoring our God. It's more than a title; it's about honoring God. It's more than a position; it's honoring God. Fruit born from death in Christ does that. It's not the clear, measurable results of a man's work that justifies both him and his work before God; it is the degree of honor the man and his work give to the Lord.

Each Christian is building something with his/her life on the foundation of Christ, and slipshod workmanship is not acceptable.[2] We must be careful of two things: first, the materials we use and second, the quality of our work. The judgment of Christ will reveal whether all the deeds of the saints are gold, silver, and precious jewels, or wood, hay, and stubble. It may be hard to tell the difference now. It won't be then! On that day everyone will be able to spot the works that give honor to Him: the ones that survive the fire. That poof of smoke wafting its way upward? We know what those were.

---

[1] John 12:24
[2] 1 Corinthians 3:12

> The work of each [one] will become [plainly, openly] known (shown for what it is); for the day [of Christ] will disclose and declare it, because it will be revealed with fire, and the fire will test and critically appraise the character and worth of the work each person has done.[3]

Many times our sense of success and productivity is based upon our commitment to a project, a position, or maintaining a title rather than honor to God. Far more than we wish to admit, those of us who have been working in the church for a long time have seen that when the position goes, the person goes. It really wasn't about serving and honoring God at all. For some their presence in the church continues only because of the position they have protected. The appearance is that they are only serious about life in the church as long as they can keep the title of *something*.

You know what they are *like* with the title, but what are they like *without* it? The real character of a person is revealed not when he is given a title but when he has a title removed. Take away the title and suddenly he is no longer the same person. That previously upbeat person now reflects gloom and doom; he has "victim" written all over himself. He comes to church less enthusiastically. Suddenly the pastor's sermons are no longer palatable. He is not being fed. Giving? Forget

---

[3] 1 Corinthians 3:13

it. As far as he's concerned, since he no longer has a position in the church, why should he be there? So he's not.

God's Primary Prerequisite

When God puts His finger on a person's life and commissions him or her to a specific, meaningful assignment, the *first* qualification for which He is looking is the condition of that person's heart. *That is not the first thing we look for.* When God sent Samuel to anoint a king replacement for Saul, he sent him to Jesse's house. The prophet was convinced Jesse's first son, Eliab, had to be the perfect choice. But God rejected him. The reason? His heart wasn't right. Outwardly, he had a very attractive appearance, every appealing physical attribute, everything that was pleasing to the eye—but God was looking deeper. What God was looking for was not quite so obvious.

He was looking at his heart, not his stage presence.

Productivity, results, and success have become trademarks that identify the forward-thinking, proactive, in-tune, in-step progressive preacher/church of this generation. Numbers have been given disproportionate value in determining the success of a ministry. Two seemingly innocent questions have been the most significant definers of church success the past thirty years. The first, "How big is it?" The second, "How fast did it happen?" Neither question even begins to touch on what is important to God. Am I anti-big, anti-numbers, or anti-big offerings? Not at all! But I am anti-using-the-wrong-things-to-measure-success-in-the-kingdom-of-God!

The church of America has set itself up for deception. We have put on equal footing *character and competence*. In the kingdom of God, they are *not* equal. Character will always be given more value than competence. God will always do more of *eternal value* with a pure heart than He will with a skilled hand. What we need is a renewed revelation of what success means to Him. Because we honor competence over character, we keep ignoring all the signs of character lack because that person is so good and so talented. My, how gifted! Besides, if we actually expect her to live godly as well as be talented, why, she just might get offended and go to the highest bidder down the street! So we justify, excuse, and ignore all the character lack so the program doesn't decline. Honor men, dishonor God.

A unique blessing of God rests upon the person who can with beggarly humility come to Jesus, knowing he is worthless apart from Him, knowing he is useless in and of himself, and who can graciously accept the idea that he can live and work the rest of his life absolutely unnoticed. Jesus blesses the man whose first and primary characteristic is that he knows he is sadly deficient! When those who are poor in spirit come to Him, they *are accepted, not rejected.* When those who are poor in spirit come to Him, they are empowered to be salt and do good works, *not disqualified from use.*

Cultural Deformity

I am convinced the greatest danger in the church is not sexual addiction but success addiction. With our need to succeed, we have embraced, endorsed, and encouraged flesh-driven forms of success that merely stockpile fuel for the coming fire that will reveal the true nature of all our works. Poof! This deceptive kind of success decided by our culture embraces showmanship rather than seeking true anointing that is found in brokenness. This deceptive kind of success endorses flesh-driven competition rather than broken and contrite servanthood. This deceptive kind of success encourages a strategy birthed by the culture of corporate America rather than one birthed while waiting before God: simply hearing and obeying.

To embrace a form of success sculpted by our culture is to reduce the majesty and splendor of true servanthood to some empty, carnal, and earthly definition. If results, success, and productivity are the only legitimate validators to identify a person truly called of God, is that to say God only opens doors, He never closes one? Is it to say that the person who goes forth weeping bearing precious seed is just out of luck?

Not all callings are the joy of harvesting. The closed door is as much God's providence as the open door; it is equally used to bring honor to His name while accomplishing His own sometimes mysterious and wonderful ends. Shall we diminish the man of contrite spirit who cares little about earthly success, but who with great passion before men and before principalities exalts the Lord? The weeping sower and the rejoicing harvester equally honor our God and Father.

God Requires Less

I have said little about skills, gifts, talents, and abilities. But please do *not* interpret that lack of emphasis as a lack of importance. God is the giver of talents and skills He distributes by His own mysterious choosing. He also has a *lot* to say about lazy, slothful, and negligent workers. It's *not* an either-or issue. What shall I choose: my heart or my gift? That's not it at all.

It is a matter of sequence. It's first things first. In the kingdom of God, it is always character first, abilities second. Just get the order right and kingdom success follows. If character is not right, God *will not* be honored by the works done, regardless of how much applause they receive from men. Jesus said, *"This is to my Father's glory, that you bear much fruit..."*[4] That sounds a lot like results, success, and productivity to me! So, doesn't that contradict everything I just said? Let's see.

---

[4] John 15:8

There is a divine sequence in Jesus's teaching in John 15 that leads us to the glorifying and honoring of God.

- You must submit to a pruning process (2).
- You must abide in me (4).
- That process results in a lot of fruit (5).
- The "lot of fruit" brings honor to My Father (8).

The word Jesus uses for "abide-remain"[5] means *"to stay in place."* It is so important to the lot-of-fruit (which we want) and the honor to His Father (which Jesus wants) that He uses the word seven times in eight verses. When is it most important *"to stay in place"*? When you are being pruned! When God determines something needs to be cut out of your life! We want to go straight to the much fruit and skip the most important part of success and productivity in the kingdom.

The production of much fruit and the resultant honor to God *only* happens if I stay still and allow Him to cut *me*. You cannot run away from God's cutting and bear the kind of fruit He is looking for. You pray for grace and stand still. Here's the sequence: the less of me, the more fruit. Believe it or not, less is more. Mark this: the sole purpose of the branch is to give the vine a channel to flow through; the branch exists solely for the vine to use.

---

[5] Greek: *meno*—stay in place.

What about me? What do I get? Sooner or later we will always come to that question. Don't see that as selfish! God expects results in His own efforts[6]—and He made us to want results to our efforts as well! When you humble yourself before God and stay in place rather than running from His pruning process, the personal benefits are staggering:

- Unlimited devotion equals unlimited access to God.
- The person who gives everything for God can claim everything from God.
- The person who is ready to risk everything for God can count on God to do everything for him.

Somewhere in the pruning process, you will struggle with being broken, struggle with your will, struggle with your emotions, and struggle with your ambitions. Somewhere in here you will struggle with total surrender. Somewhere in here you will come face-to-face with trusting God. All of that is the Gardener doing His pruning—cutting away all the things that look good to you that sound appealing...but produce *nothing*! The *position*: be a branch. The *process*: pruning. The *results: priceless*.

God Requires Truth

Do you remember when Gideon had gathered thousands and thousands and thousands of people to fight the

---

[6] Isaiah 55:8–10

Midianites?[7] Do you know why God rejected 99 percent of them? In his strategic planning session with Gideon, God said to him, "You have too many people." When Gideon heard that, he must have been shocked! How can you have too many men when you go to war? Thirty-two thousand men had responded to his call to arms and General Gideon was feeling pretty good about their chances. Yet, God said that's too many. But there is a specific reason why God rejected this large number of men.

> In order that Israel may not boast against me that her own strength has saved her.[8]

Was God showing His displeasure at the large turnout? No. Is God into small? No. God *is into* His work being done His way: a way that gives all honor to Him…to Him alone. They hadn't done anything yet—not a single spear, arrow, or rock had been launched in anger! There had not yet been any bragging because there had not been any victory about which to brag! But they were *going* to do it and God knew it.

The Old Testament Hebrew word used in this passage of Judges 7, *"boast,"* appears to be extremely twenty-first-century contemporary. It carries the clear meaning *"to embellish."* To exaggerate. To stretch the truth. Today we

---

[7] Judges 7
[8] Judges 7:2

chuckle when people say, "I'm speaking evangelistically." But we know what they're really saying, "Well, what I just said is not *exactly* the truth." In fact, it may be far from the truth. They just simply gave us a heads-up, an advance notice that they were embellishing a fact, a story, *emphasizing something to make it sound better.* Usually to make *them* look better.

God is not into embellishing! He doesn't need you to make something more spectacular, more sensational than it really is. In some misguided attempt to let people know how "God showed up," we have this perverted idea that if we make it sound better, we are really honoring Him. But we aren't. We are honoring ourselves! It makes *me* look better. More anointed than I am. More talented than I am. More wise than I am. More of a warrior than I am. More of a threat to hell than I am. It's back to the battle in heaven, and this time I'm the one out to steal God's honor.

*As strange it seems, God is quite content with just the **truth**.*

God *knows* the person who engages in any form of ministry and who does it for the wrong reason. He *knows* if you are in the ministry, and stay in, to make a good living. He *knows* if you are in the ministry because you love the power and authority. He *knows* if you are in the ministry because you love the money. He *knows* if you are in the ministry primarily because you get a lot of attention.

I can say with absolute certainty the person in for the wrong reason *will* embellish…and God *will not* be honored. But this I also know: I will give an account for my own heart. I will give an account to Him who knows thoughts, imaginations, and intentions. I will explain to Him why I had the audacity to take His honor for myself. It doesn't matter if my ministry could be described as highly visible, attention-getting, a streaking meteor, or the opposite, like flying in stealth mode, out of sight, and not even on the radar. Myself, and every other believer (without exception), will have our works pass through that fire that defines motive. There goes another poof of smoke. God have mercy on us if we have touched His glory.

Seeds of Need

The things done in the name of the Lord that most significantly impact eternity, that go far beyond obvious productivity, obvious results, and obvious success, are first and foremost a matter of the heart. Is your heart right? Is your heart pure? Are there seeds of need: the need-to-look-good, the need-to-be-recognized, the need-to-be-accepted, the need-to-be-successful, the need-to-get-attention that have been planted in your heart but may not have had opportunity to grow today, but will grow tomorrow?

Heaven really does pay attention to what's going on. In Jeremiah's day the prophets and priests were basking in real success. They weren't seeing many people transformed or set free, but hey, they were rubbing shoulders with all the people of influence and getting rich in the process. All the while, behind the scenes, God was whispering some real truth to Jeremiah:

> They have tired themselves out but profit nothing. They shall be ashamed of their harvests...[9]

Ouch!

The real measuring device for all we produce is not found in numbers alone, not in high visibility, not in having some international reputation, not in some corporate definition of success. The true measuring stick will always be found in this question: *Did it bring honor to God?* We are prone to set results, success, and productivity as the target of Christian service; how disappointing. Those are goals set by modern culture and are not by the design of the Spirit. The real aim for every believer, especially those of us in leadership roles, ought to be to honor and glorify our God through human expression.

If results are my goal, sooner or later, I am going to find a way to justify doing things in ways that are neither spiritual nor God honoring. It's one thing to produce results; it's quite another to consider *how* I produced them. Maybe our

---

[9] Jeremiah 12:13

passion needs to be adjusted. What if we were set on fire with a passion to *just honor God*! What would happen if we pushed success to the back burner and our hearts were set on fire to *just honor God*? Is it possible we just don't think hard enough or care deeply enough about His honor?

Strangely enough, some of the things that give God honor are things He doesn't even allow us to do, or dreams we have that never become reality. There may be deep passions that are not realized in our lifetime. David is an example. He had always wished to build the temple of God, to build God a house much finer than David's own palace. He could see it. He had a plan. He had the means to make it happen, but he never achieved that noble ambition; his request was denied.

> But the Lord said to David my father, "whereas it was in your heart to build a house unto my name, you did well that it was in your heart."[10]

How fantastic it is that God judges us, not only by our achievements but also by our dreams: *"You did well that it was in your heart."* How encouraging that is. I just love that! I don't think this was just a wistful passing thought David had—sort of a "wouldn't it be nice to" kind of thing. How do I know? Because even after he was told he wouldn't be

---

[10] 1 Kings 8:18

allowed to fulfill his heart's dream, he poured himself into doing everything in his vast power to help the person who *would* be allowed to do it!

What a novel idea! Help someone else do what God won't let me do. Help someone else produce the results. Let them get the credit. If it's really all about *His* honor, why am I so protective and possessively afraid someone will steal *my* idea? I just may not get to do "this," so does that mean "this" shouldn't get done!

Holy Spirit, make *me* passionate about His honor!

> The twin deceivers of the Christian life are success and failure. God has called us to neither. He has called us to faithfulness.
>
> Oswald Chambers

"To worship is to quicken the
conscience by the holiness
of God, to feed the mind
with the truth of God,
to pursue the imagination
by the beauty of God,
to open the heart to the love
of God, to devote the will
to the purpose of God."

William Temple
Archbishop of Canterbury

· 10 ·

Befitting Your Majesty

In the end, a believer's great pursuit in life must go much farther and deeper than the pursuit of greater faith—even more than learning how to claim and appropriate God's promises. The ultimate pursuit must be a life that brings honor to God. Whether living in a repressive anti-God culture in the first century that made Christians criminals or an anti-God culture in the twenty-first century rapidly moving toward making Christianity illegal, a believer's primary concern ought to be living in a manner befitting His majesty.

While living in a culture where society is submerged in a sea of sexual pleasure and material gain, a believer's primary concern *still ought* to be living in a manner befitting His majesty. But it is more easily said than done. We are surrounded by unseen powers and principalities that have a history of warring against God and His majesty that predates creation and time itself. Consequently, they have far more experience in promoting dishonor to God than we have in trying to honor Him.

War in Heaven

Can three words possibly be any more incongruous than these three: war in heaven? Something seems amiss in that statement; something seems out of sync. How can there be war in the place of ultimate peace? Jealousy and envy...*in heaven*? Strife and anger...*in heaven*? Division and rebellion ...*in heaven*? Animosity, belligerence, wrath, gossip, lying... *in heaven*? *War in heaven?*

This is war at a magnitude we simply cannot fathom in a place we would least expect. Started by whom? Started for what reason? This war didn't *just* happen. It was a long time in the making, but when it happened, it impacted every single created being there. And since that great conflict, every single mortal being here on earth has been touched by it. You have been influenced by this war; I have been influenced by this war...and we weren't even there when it started. What happened before the cosmos was created is extremely relevant. It is not just ancient history; it is as current as today's news. Let me repeat, it is extremely personal to you and me.

Isaiah, Ezekiel, Peter, and John[1] leave no doubt as to the instigator/provocateur of this tragedy...Satan. From the middle ages to the present, Christian tradition has identified him as "Lucifer" in both OT and NT writings. He is described as the most beautiful and the most exquisite of all God's handiwork. Why did Lucifer do this thing? Most of what theologians write concerning Lucifer's motives for leading this

---

[1] Isaiah 14, Ezekiel 28, 2 Peter 2, Revelation 12

uprising indicate pride was the reason—a vain pride in his beauty and even more pride in his position. But was pride the *real* issue? Not exactly; there was more—much more.

Pride was only a *catalyst* for Lucifer. Let me suggest this analogy: pride was like a vehicle you use to transport you to where you want to go—not your destination, just the means to get there. It was like an accelerator you use to begin a huge fire—not the fire, just the means to start it. His pride had a precise objective, because *pride is never the ultimate objective in and of itself.* It is not, "I want pride just so I can have pride."

Pride has a wicked, voracious appetite for *specific things*: recognition, attention, status. Something seen as an exalting benefit to "self" is being pursued; *that* is what pride is really after. In Lucifer's case he wanted one thing above everything else: honor. For Lucifer, he pursued his objective through the means of war because he couldn't get what he wanted, or make the changes he wanted to make, lawfully, rightly, or honorably.

The inherent motive to his unbridled pride, the objective to which his pride drove him, was to possess *the honor that was being given to God*—supreme honor. There is a certain element of mystery that surrounds all that took place prior to and during that war. Some of it we "see through a glass darkly," but one thing is certain: Lucifer wanted to replace

God and become the center of all honor, all glory, and all majesty and the object of all worship.

War on Earth

In the last two generations there has been a distinct erosion of honor that transcends continents and cultures. My travels take me around the world…and I ask a lot of questions. I ask questions of people who are old enough, who have been around long enough, and who have seen enough of these cultural changes. Honor is in such short supply we hardly understand the meaning of it anymore. In many historical cultures and clans honor was once the "glue" that held them together when other powers were trying to tear them apart. Cultures once widely known for the place honor held among its peoples are becoming less and less identified in that way. Now we have become a worldwide people who specialize in dishonor.

Honor has now taken on a singular definition that is determined by behavior. *Not your position, but your performance.* As long as you perform in the manner I want you to, I praise you; as long as you do things that I agree with, I brag on you; as long as your behavior makes sense to me and is what I expect, I honor you. But once you stop performing like I want you to, stop making decisions with which I agree, or you disagree with me once too often, suddenly you become suspect. Your character comes into question, and the honor previously given to you suddenly vanishes. I now look at you with jaded eyes that are quick to dishonor you.

All too often we do the same toward God. As long as He "performs" like we think He should, all is well. But when He too frequently does the opposite of our expectations, we begin to question His character and His Word. We grieve, we lament, we beg, and we implore that God do the right thing, which is to perform to our expectations. If He does not, we stop honoring Him by his position and we dishonor Him because of His poor *performance*.

The stealing of honor for my "self" (though I may attempt to justify my actions) is a dangerous thing in which to be engaged. Living a life that does not honor God simply does not end well. The Scripture links the two components, pride and dishonor, in an inseparable way.

> When pride comes, then comes shame (*Qalown*: dishonor)...[2]

> A man's pride brings him low, but a man of lowly spirit gains honor.[3]

---

[2] Proverbs 11:2 MEV
[3] Proverbs. 11:29

No wonder God warns us so much about pride. It's dangerous! Nothing good comes from it. Pride was the catalyst for
war in heaven, and this deceptive form of self-honor is at the
top of the list of things God hates. When you read the short
list of things God hates (Proverbs 6), you find the first item
on God's despised list is a *"proud look."* The deception of
pride is so blinding. For example, one thing that is not much
of a mystery is the significant list of things Lucifer had given
to him when God created him:

- He was recognized as the greatest of all angels.
- He was given a prominent position.
- He was given a title.
- He was given authority.
- He had great influence.
- He was the most beautiful thing God ever made.
- He was given this world as his possession.
- He was given his own kingdom.
- He was given his own throne.

Things Will Never Be the Same
That's an impressive list, but Lucifer's pride told him it was
not enough; Lucifer wanted more. He wanted to be *supreme*
in *all categories*. And the only way to have the highest honor,
supreme honor, was to exalt his throne above God's throne.
Make no mistake about it, the war in heaven was about
honor: God's honor. Since the failure of Lucifer's militant

overthrow and challenge to steal His honor, God has made two significant changes:

1. *God no longer chooses to work through the powerful and mighty.*

> But God chose what is foolish in the world to shame the wise; God chose what is weak in the world to shame the strong; God chose what is low and despised in the world, even things that are not, to bring to nothing things that are, so that no human being might boast in the presence of God.[4]

The very thing God chooses, we now so desperately try to camouflage: weakness. We spend agonizing years with intense focus trying to rid ourselves of the very trait that makes us acceptable to Him. The first thing Jesus blessed in His Sermon on the Mount was the person who recognized they had nothing to offer God: "Blessed are the poor in spirit, for theirs is the kingdom of heaven."[5] There are two Greek words for "poor." This one is the most extreme; it means to have nothing, absolutely nothing. Not just to have little: to have nothing. It brings redemptive blessing to the person who embraces the abject poverty of man and the unspeakable riches of God's grace. God rejects our phony fullness, not our obvious poverty.

---

[4] 1 Corinthians 1:27–29 ESV
[5] Matthew 5:3

Writing to his son in the faith, Timothy, Paul expresses his thankfulness to the Lord for "believing in me," "trusting me," and "appointing me," even though he had formerly been "a blasphemer," "a persecutor," and "violent." Paul went on in the same passage to say, "I am the chief of sinners."[6] Why would Paul want to so vividly remember his own sin? Would you not want to forget what you were before Christ and focus on the new man you now are becoming in Christ? This is not the only place in his writings where Paul recalls his past life; it's clear he intends no cover-up. Why?

Paul's sin was not something he tried to forget; it was something he *refused* to forget! It was not that he sat around in some morbid and unhealthy brood over his past life; it was that Paul remembered his sin to keep alive and relevant a *humble thankfulness to the greatness of God's mercy and grace!*

- The memory of his sin was a sure way to keep him from pride.
- Those memories kept him forever filled with gratitude.
- Recalling his own sin was an encouragement to others that God's grace would certainly cover theirs.

---

[6] 1 Timothy 1:12–17

We tend to forget God's people (whether for good or bad) are compared to a variety of things in the natural world, including weak things:

- as a dove among fowl
- as a vine among trees
- as a sheep among wolves
- as a smoking flax is to fire
- as a bruised reed is to a temple pillar

In the present church mind-set, Christians are discouraged from even thinking of being weak; we are most commonly taught to declare we are:

- an eagle, not a dove
- an oak, not a vine
- a lion, not a sheep
- a warrior, not a bride
- a raging fire, not a wisp of smoke

However, the journey is not that clear, not that well defined. This generation embraces the false perception that for one's life to be honorable, it must always demonstrate strength. Weakness is not an option. Discouragement is not an option. Fear is not an option. Who said so? Not God! Not Paul!

When I am weak…then I am strong.

God has chosen the weak...that no human being should glory.

Here is the rub. There is no inherent glory in strength, and there is no inherent shame in weakness! The glory is in *Him!* We all will have both strength and weakness in varying seasons of our journey. Therefore, the object of our pursuit should be neither to maximize strength or stick your head in the sand and deny your weakness; it should be a life lived befitting His majesty.

2. *The magnitude of honor and excellence God gave to Lucifer has never again been given to a created being.*

But we have this treasure in jars of clay to show that this all-surpassing power is from God and not from us.[7]

Isn't it interesting that God will give to any man or woman:

- His grace
- His mercy
- His love
- His faithfulness
- His provision
- His mind
- His authority

---

[7] 2 Corinthians 4:7 NIV

- His power
- His life
- His patience
- His peace
- His righteousness
- His presence
- His attention
- His Spirit
- His Son

But He will not give any man or woman His *honor*! He wouldn't relinquish it to Satan in the great war in heaven, and He will not yield or give it up to any person here on earth. God's honor is of ultimate importance to Him, and it must become so to us! God doesn't stammer, stutter, or hesitate when addressing this subject:

I am the Lord; that is my name! *I will not give my glory to another...*[8]

For my own sake, for my own sake I do this. How can I let myself be defamed? *I will not yield my glory to another.*[9]

But I had concern for my name, which the house of Israel had profaned among the nations to which they came.

---

[8] Isaiah 42:8
[9] Isaiah 48:11

Therefore say to the house of Israel, Thus says the Lord
God: It is not for your sake, O house of Israel, that I am
about to act, but for the sake of my holy name, *which you
have profaned* among the nations to which you came.[10]

Our Gross Misunderstanding

To accurately capture how important His own honor is to
God Himself, we must at least briefly consider two phrases
found over and over in both the OT and NT: *"for your name's
sake"* and *"for my name's sake."* These phrases, whether
in Hebrew or Greek, mean the exact same thing: first, it
encapsulates the honor, authority, and dignity that are held
in the person's name; second, it reveals and makes known
the whole nature and character of that person.

So, so, so many of the things God does for us we *think* are
done for our benefit. But the *greater truth* is that they are
not. They are done for His honor!

- God does not forsake His people—not because we His
  people are so deserving...*but for His name's sake*
  (1 Sam.12:22).
- God leads us in paths of righteousness—not just so we
  can walk the straight and narrow...*but for His name's
  sake* (Ps. 23:3).

---

[10] Ezekiel 36:21–22

- We have the right to appeal for pardon when we sin—
  not just to ease our guilty conscience...*but for His name's
  sake* (Ps. 25:11).
- He leads me and guides me—not just so I don't get lost
  or so I don't get into trouble...*but for His name's sake*
  (Ps. 31:3).
- We can expect Him to help us, deliver us—not just
  because we need it...*but for His name's sake* (Ps. 79:9).
- God delivered Israel at the Red Sea—because they were
  such faith-filled people? No...*but for His name's sake*
  (Ps.106:8).
- It goes on and on in both the OT and the NT.
  He delivers...*but for His name's sake.*
  He does good...*but for His name's sake.*
  He preserves from destruction...*but for His name's sake.*
  He defers His anger...*but for His name's sake.*
  He does not break covenant...*but for His name's sake.*

Let me give you one more (there are far too many to list),
but just one more, *"our sins are forgiven for His name's
sake."* [11] That may cause you to rethink your theology! Sins
are forgiven *primarily* for **His name's sake**.

From the time of Lucifer's rebellion in heaven, to the present
raging of nations, God's character has been maligned. But
the name of the Father and the Son *will* be honored!

---

[11] 1 John 2:12

> Therefore God exalted him to the highest place and gave him the name that is above every name, that at the name of Jesus every knee should bow, in heaven and on earth and under the earth, and every tongue acknowledge that Jesus Christ is Lord, *to the glory of God the Father.*[12]

> The name of the LORD is a strong tower; the righteous man runs into it and is safe.[13]

> Some trust in horses, some in chariots, but we trust in *the name of the Lord our God...*[14]

If we know His name, not merely that it is Jehovah or Jesus, *but that it stands for full disclosure of His nature and character*, we will use it, which He desires us to do and we will honor it, which He demands us to do. Beyond the mind and beyond logic, there is an *understanding in the spirit* of the reborn that it's all about His honor. When your heart is full, when deep is crying unto deep, when your very soul is engaged in His presence, when it seems like you will burst if you don't cry out...*then* there is a spontaneous eruption that comes pouring out of your heart with a voice of powerful adoration:

---

[12] Philippians 2:9–11
[13] Proverbs 18:10
[14] Psalm 20:7

We exalt you, O Lord!
We bless you, Father!
We glorify your name, O Lord!
We honor you today, O God!

What we sing and shout is not unlike the scenes in heaven. The tension, strife, and rebellion of Satan's war are gone forever, replaced with willing glory and honor to the only One deserving of such:

> Worthy is the Lamb, who was slain, to receive power and wealth and wisdom and strength and honor and glory and praise! Then I heard every creature in heaven and on earth and under the earth and on the sea, and all that is in them, saying: To Him who sits on the throne and to the Lamb be praise and honor and glory and power forever and ever![15]

Now to the King eternal, immortal, invisible, the only God, be honor and glory for ever and ever. Amen.

---

[15] Revelation 5:11–13

About the Author

Jim Mackey is a respected counselor, pastor, adjunct professor and international teacher. While engaged in pastoring a local church, he and his wife, Lynette, founded Shepherd Springs Ministries in 1978, a trans-denominational service ministry to clergy and clergy families. Their passion for the well-being of clergy families has taken them into well over thirty countries on five continents. For ten years, Shepherd Springs served as a referral ministry with Focus on the Family for pastor families in Texas.

Since 2008, Dr. Mackey has served as an adjunct professor of theology and New Testament studies at Christ for the Nations in Dallas, TX, and has served as an adjunct professor at The King's University in Southlake, TX. He is also a permanent member of *Theta Kappa Alpha*, The National Honor Society for Religious Studies and Theology.

His ministry has been varied and well-traveled, spanning over five decades. Jim and Lynette have worked with pastors in Asia since 1988 and have established two schools for house church pastors in China. In Nigeria they have established three regional pastor schools, one Bible Institute and two elementary schools.

Dr. Mackey has a B.S. in Religious Education from Southwestern Assemblies of God University, graduate work in psychology at Northern Arizona University, an M.A. in Theological Studies from Southwestern Assemblies of God University, and a D.Min. from Andersonville Theological Seminary.

Jim and Lynette have three children and ten grandchildren.